Antiques 101

A CRASH COURSE IN EVERYTHING ANTIQUE

FRANK FARMER LOOMIS IV

©2005 Frank Farmer Loomis IV

Published by

kp books
An Imprint of F+W Publications

700 East State Street • Iola, WI 54990-0001
715-445-2214 • 888-457-2873

Our toll-free number to place an order or obtain
a free catalog is (800) 258-0929.

Library of Congress Catalog Number: 2005930193

ISBN: 0-89689-158-5

Designed by Sandy Kent
Edited by Dan Brownell

Printed in Canada

Cover photo: table model disc
phonograph, circa early 1900s.

Dedication

These wonderful people are my heroes. This book is dedicated to them with friendship and gratitude: Dan Brownell, Janet Costa, William Hahn, Lee Hay, Paul Kennedy, Rick McCrabb and Thomas Oder.

Acknowledgments

I would like to thank the following for their generous contribution of photographs:

- Cincinnati Art Museum, Cincinnati, Ohio
- Du Mouchelle's Auction, Detroit, Michigan
- Early Auction Company, Milford, Ohio
- Forsythes' Auctions, Cincinnati, Ohio
- Garth's Auctions, Inc., Delaware, Ohio
- Howard's Wood Products, Paso Robles, California
- Jackson's International Auctions, Cedar Falls, Iowa
- Skinner Auctions, Inc., Boston, Massachusetts
- Tim and Kathy Tyler, Cincinnati, Ohio
- Treadway Toomey Galleries, Cincinnati, Ohio, and Oak Park, Illinois
- Wooden Nickel Antiques, Cincinnati, Ohio

Contents

SECTION THREE

Antiques Classics | 196

SECTION FOUR

Antiques Legends | 238

SECTION FIVE

Antiques Superstars | 266

SECTION SIX

Preparing for Graduation | 286

A Timeline of Style

PERIOD	APPROXIMATE DATE
QUEEN ANNE	(1720ISH - 1760ISH)
CHIPPENDALE	(1750 - 1780ISH)
HEPPLETON	(1790S - 1820ISH)
EMPIRE	(1800ISH - 1850)
ROCOCO REVIVAL	(1850 - 1870)
EASTLAKE	(1870 - 1890)
RENAISSANCE REVIVAL	(1880 - 1890S)
AESTHETIC MOVEMENT	(1880S - 1890S)
CENTENNIAL REPRODUCTIONS	(1880S - 1890S)
ART NOUVEAU I	(1890ISH - 1905ISH)
ART NOUVEAU II	(1900ISH - 1915ISH)
ARTS AND CRAFTS	(1900ISH - 1920ISH)
ART DECO	(1920S)
ART DECO II	(1930ISH - 1950ISH)
MID CENTURY	(1950S AND 1960S)
RETRO	(1970S - 1980S)

BACKGROUND HISTORICAL EVENTS

FRANCE CEDES CANADA TO GREAT BRITAIN

THE AMERICAN REVOLUTION

THE WAR OF 1812

THE WAR OF 1812/WESTERN EXPANSION

THE U.S. CIVIL WAR

RECONSTRUCTION AND THE CENTENNIAL

BIRTH OF THE SKYSCRAPER/GROWTH OF U.S. CITIES

BIRTH OF THE SKYSCRAPER/GROWTH OF U.S. CITIES

BIRTH OF THE SKYSCRAPER/GROWTH OF U.S. CITIES

THE DEATH OF QUEEN VICTORIA

THE PARIS WORLD'S FAIR OF 1900

WORLD WAR I

THE ROARING TWENTIES

THE GREAT DEPRESSION/WORLD WAR II

I LOVE LUCY AND THE BEATLES

THE U.S. BICENTENNIAL

SECTION ONE

❧ ❧

An Introduction to Antiques

Chapter 1

What Does Elvis Have To Do With Antiques?

A decade ago in my antiques classes at the University of Cincinnati, my students and I discussed how age and handcraftsmanship don't always guarantee quality. To illustrate that point, I routinely commented that although velvet Elvis Presley paintings are handmade, they aren't necessarily first class. But I would never make such a statement about these paintings now because Elvis is more stellar than ever, and something extraordinary has happened to those fabric portraits. "El on Vel," as I affectionately call this genre, has become a new category of antiques that many collectors find "awesome." The King is only one of the numerous examples of how our perception of value changes over time.

Let me tell you what a delight it is to welcome you to the wonderful world of antiques! You are on the threshold of an exciting adventure. *Antiques 101* will help make you a savvy antiquer and a better person, too. As you read this primer, I promise:

- You'll be pleasantly surprised by the perks that antiques provide.
- The major furniture styles will become second nature to you.
- The main woods used in antique furniture will become more familiar to your fingers than the keys of your computer.
- You'll learn to distinguish French Limoges porcelain from English Wedgwood services.
- You'll become astute at differentiating solid silver from plated pieces.
- You'll be able to tell molded from cut glass by touch.
- Movies will be even more enjoyable because you'll relish the furnishings as plots unfold.
- Museums will become favorite destinations because you'll be

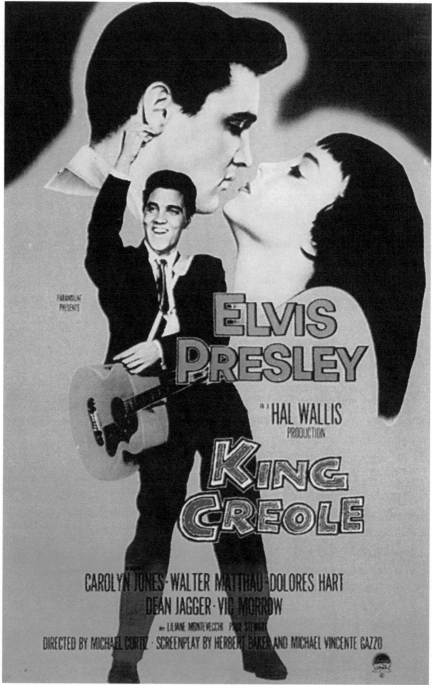

Elvis is the King of Retro as well as the King of Rock.

able to view out-of-this-world artifacts in their collections.
* You'll be able to spot unappreciated treasures passed over by other antiquers at garage sales, flea markets, shows, shops and malls.
* You'll experience firsthand that "Knowledge is Power."

Get ready to add antiques to the list of things that—like pets, music, exercise, sunshine and loved ones—bring joy to our lives. Pardon my gushiness about antiques, but my enthusiasm is sincere. You see, my whole life revolves around antiques—always has and always will.

Your Antiques Coach's Credentials

Before we delve into basic antiques terminology, I would like to tell you a little about my background. Just think of me as your antiques coach, since I truly regard antiques as a sport, and you will, too.

While other kids were playing baseball or other sports, I was happily trekking to auctions near and far with my wonderful antiquer Aunt Panny. It just never occurred to me that I was missing out on athletics, because I have always regarded antiquing as a game. You see, antiquing, like more traditional sports, involves exercise, practice, timing and even proper attire. Although scouting for antiques may not seem as vigorous as football or tennis, it is a physical activity benefiting body, mind and home.

A musical photo album from the late 1800s demonstrates Victorian love for ornateness.

As an adult, my passion for antiques took over my professional life. After earning a graduate degree in French, I opened a small antiques shop, which I operated for a few years. And for more than 25 years since then, I have been a full-time, independent appraiser of antiques (which means I don't buy what I appraise). During those years, I have written books and syndicated newspaper columns, had my own television and radio shows, and frequently do speaking engagements. In addition, as I pointed out earlier, I teach antiques classes at the University of Cincinnati, which is one of the great delights of my career.

To tell the truth, many ideas in this book have come from my grand students and listeners who call me on my radio show *Keep Antiquing!* on WVXU in Cincinnati. What a joy to meet folks like you. Recently,

Antique 1920s radios such as this RCA Radiola-Victrola combined music with fine cabinetry.

Forsythes' Auctions

at a favorite mall, a former student told me how my classes changed her life. She explained that she gave up her career as a physical education instructor to make her living selling antiques. To be frank, (no pun intended), that scared me a little, but Amy was truly grateful and added a cheerful "Thanks!" Her success is another example of how antiques are indeed a sport enriching our lives in many marvelous ways.

My renaissance background in antiques allows me to present a knowledgeable and unbiased perspective from various points of view—dealer, appraiser, collector, writer, instructor, and television and radio host. This means that when I discuss a particular style or design, I don't let my personal preferences sway my coaching. (Well, when we get to one particular design that is my very favorite, I am professional enough to declare my partiality.) My varied and hands-on experience makes me an excellent coach for beginning antiquers.

Loomisms Just for You

My goal is to make your learning as pleasant as taking a stroll on a sunny day. I know what you will be going through because I had to master the same information, so I will avoid fancy terminology and instead offer "Loomisms," which are simple maxims I have developed over a lifetime of experience. They're practical, concise and memorable enough for instant recall as you go antiquing. But enough of your antiques coach; let's get right to learning.

Antiques Terminology

Your first step is to familiarize yourself with collecting terminology. Even though the definition of "antique" can be as perplexing and intimidating as programming your cell phone, you have nothing to dread. I will demystify all the perplexing twaddle for you. So here's how we define the elusive term "antique."

Skinner Auctions, Inc.

This 1956 Ford Thunderbird coupe rocks!

The Antique Meaning of "Antiques"

For centuries "antique" referred to artifacts from Greek, Roman or Egyptian times, which were only affordable to well-heeled connoisseurs. Today, when museums or auction houses refer to relics from those ancient civilizations, they describe them as "antiquities."

Treadway Toomey Galleries

These walnut cabinets made by Herman Miller are as up-to-date as if they were made yesterday but actually date from the mid-20th century.

Curios

As collecting became increasingly popular in the 1800s, the middle class eagerly accumulated less costly items from more recent times. Artifacts from ancient civilizations were still called antiques, while younger relics from the 1600s and 1700s were charmingly called "curios." Charles Dickens cleverly wove these curios into the plot of his 1840 best-selling novel *The Old Curiosity Shop*, which tells the story of Nell Trent and her grandfather, who owned a second-hand store.

In Victorian days, the curio cabinet, a piece of furniture once found primarily in museums, became a common parlor piece. Etageres, or "whatnot" shelves, crammed with small objects known as bric-a-brac, were Victorian everyday versions of curio cabinets.

In the 1890s, the term "antique" still applied to ancient artifacts, but also began taking on the meaning it has today. If Mr. Dickens had written his novel in the early 20th century, the title would more likely have been *The Antiques Shop* than *The Old Curiosity Shop*. By then, the word "antique" had become more prevalent than "curio."

Forsythe's Auctions

Collectors love high-tech antiques like this early 1900s oak telephone booth complete with crank phone.

The Elitist Definition of "Antique"

By turn of the 20th century, it became necessary to develop a standard definition of "antique" because so many of our ancestors were buying, selling and collecting them. As a result, an early unofficial, yet universally acknowledged principle was that genuine antiques had to have been handmade and date before 1820. The Industrial Revolution was in full swing by then, marking the point when most household goods were machine-produced rather than hand-crafted. Call this doctrine the "Elitist Rule."

This 1818 bottle of French cognac falls under the pre-1820 definition of genuine antique.

Jackson's International Auctions

Two Reasons to Ignore the Elitist Rule

REASON NO. 1: The 1820 convention is too restrictive because most antiques made before then are affordable only to millionaires and big budget museums.

REASON NO. 2: If celestial prices aren't enough to steer you away from the Elitist Rule, keep in mind that being old or handmade does not guarantee quality or status. Quality is far more important than age. Just because a piece dates before 1820 doesn't mean it's first class. An item could have been poor quality from the start.

Uncle Sam's Definition of "Antique"

As the 1890s arrived, the popularity of collecting was at an all-time high. American tourists were bringing record numbers of antiques here from Europe and Asia, so the U.S. government devised a tax to protect homegrown industries. (This shows that concerns about the global economy are antique too!) By World War I, officials realized that such artifacts benefited our culture, so Uncle Sam created a more liberal ruling to encourage importation of antiques into the country. The U.S. Customs Office declared that an item 100 years old or more was antique and could enter duty free.

The First Antiques from the 20th Century, Courtesy of Uncle Sam

Obviously, according to the "100-year" rule, the definition of antique changes annually because every January first, another year qualifies for antique status. Such an adaptable and practical approach refreshes the supply of antiques, keeping prices somewhat under control.

"A Portrait of Young Boy" dating from the 1820s is a genuine antique by the Elitist Rule. In the old days, both little boys and girls wore dresses.

Skinner Auctions, Inc.

The new millennium not only ushered in a new century but an exciting era for American collectors. For the first time, goods from the early years of the 20th century are considered genuine antiques. Thanks to Uncle Sam, 1905 music boxes and oak hall stands are now the real McCoy.

The American Interpretation of "Antique"

Antiques are a bigger mania now than in the early 1900s. Ever notice the antiques shops reviving downtown areas or the antiques malls sprouting along expressways? Such antiquing havens add a whole new dimension to "rest stops" as we travel. But even with Uncle Sam's liberal 100-year rule, the number of items qualifying as antiques is not enough to keep up with demand. Therefore, my slightly revised definition of antique as pre-1920 ensures a constant supply.

A gilded copper gamecock weather vane falls under the 100 years or older definition of antique.

My date isn't arbitrary; 1920 marks a real cultural and historic shift towards the modern era. World War I ended old-fashioned traditions and kicked our high-tech lifestyle into gear. The 1920s witnessed the construction of soaring skyscrapers across America, Lindbergh's nonstop flight to Paris, knee-length dresses replacing long trailing frocks, and automobiles becoming almost as universal then as cable television is now. While this Loomism will no longer be applicable or necessary when the 1920s reaches the 100-year mark, it is appropriate now and should stay in effect until then.

Loomism

Consider anything made before 1920 as antique. This guideline keeps antiques bountiful and affordable.

Also keep in mind that where you live in the United States also affects your perception of antiques. In North America, the earliest non-Native American antiques date to the arrival of Europeans on the East Coast in the late 1500s and early 1600s. Thus, pre-1820 antiques are typically more abundant in cities like New York, Boston and Charleston. Since the remainder of America was settled later, my 1920 guideline works especially well for American and Canadian collectors who live farther West.

While the 1920 rule is great for inland collectors, it readily applies to the eastern United States too. At a recent excursion to the Atlantique City Antiques Show, billed as "The World's Largest Indoor

Antiques Show," I learned a great deal about East Coast collectors and dealers. Strolling around in antiques bliss, it occurred to me that my 1920 date works very nicely there. Fine merchandise, mostly dating after 1920, usually so dominant in Midwest and West Coast shows, also made up much of the stock at the Atlantic City, New Jersey, extravaganza. Just goes to show that pre-1820s examples are too costly for most of us, no matter where we live in the country.

The European Interpretation of "Antique"

Most Europeans have a very different viewpoint towards antiques. Their perspective really illustrates how geographic location affects the perception of "old." My visits to France have given me a great deal of insight into American concepts about antiques. We in the United

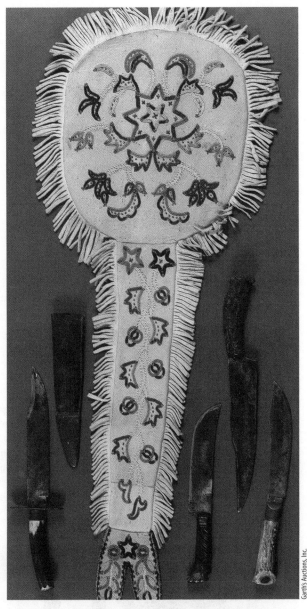

This Native American beaded case from the northern Plains dates from 1890-1900.

States can consider something antique if it dates before the 1920s. The French and other Europeans would probably get a chuckle from my interpretation, which works so well for North America. Obviously, Europeans have a different outlook because their history goes back so much further than ours. In general, Europeans only consider items made before the Industrial Revolution as genuine antiques. But if you've ever been to a European shop or outdoor show, you know that Europeans collect much the same merchandise that we Americans do—mainly early 1900s to 1950s items.

Let's return to our side of the Atlantic to learn more about the North American perspective towards antiques. Keep my 1920 date as the cut-off for genuine antiques. Now let's look at items dating after the 1920s, so highly coveted these days, to discuss the fine value they offer.

Semi-Antiques/Collectibles

What do we call items made after 1920? You'll often hear the term "collectibles" used to describe items from this era. Let's avoid this idiom; instead call these more youthful examples "semi-antiques/collectibles." Doesn't that sound more dignified? The word "collectible" just conjures up images of tube socks at flea markets. But actually, quality goods dating from the Flapper decade (the 1920s) through the World War II era are regularly displayed in flea markets, malls, shops and shows.

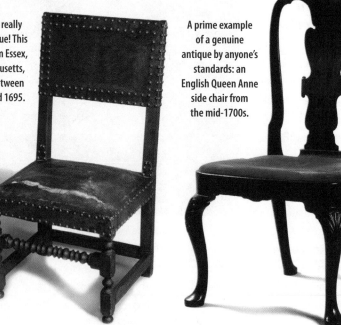

Here's a really old antique! This chair from Essex, Massachusetts, dates between 1665 and 1695.

A prime example of a genuine antique by anyone's standards: an English Queen Anne side chair from the mid-1700s.

Garth's Auctions, Inc.

Skinner Auctions, Inc.

Here is a decade-by-decade sampling of terrific semi-antiques/collectibles from the Flapper decade to the World War II years that you'll encounter in future chapters.

1920s:
- Reproductions of Queen Anne, Chippendale and other styles by fine American manufacturers
- Utilitarian Hoosier cabinets for kitchens
- Floor-model radios, early high-tech wonders

1930s:
- Curvy front bedroom suites belovedly called "Waterfall"
- Depression glass, including pitchers emblazoned with child movie star Shirley Temple
- Souvenirs from the Chicago and New York world fairs
- Roseville, McCoy and Weller ceramics

1940s:
- "Early American" furniture
- World War II memorabilia
- Cooking utensils
- "Occupied Japan" ceramics

Mid Century

In the 21st century, a major part of collecting has focused on semi-antiques/collectibles from the 1950s to the 1980s. Semi-antique/collectibles from the 1950s and '60s fall under the recently coined "Mid Century" heading and include items like the following:
- blond furniture
- big wrought iron lamps
- Formica-top kitchen tables

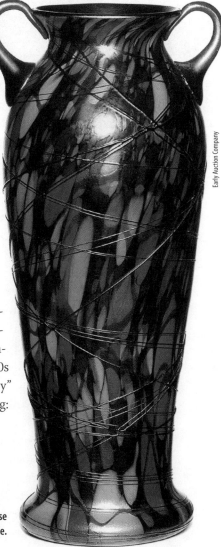

Early Auction Company

A 1926 Fenton glass mosaic two-handled vase captures the exuberance of the Flapper decade.

Karen Plunkett Powell

A vintage 1903 postcard depicting "The Old Curiosity Shop" in London, England, which in today's terminology means antiques shop.

Retro

Semi-antiques/collectibles from the 1970s and 1980s have acquired the name "Retro" and include the following goods:

- beanbag chairs
- lava lamps
- rotary telephones
- "The King" on velvet

How grand it is that the world of antiques is ever evolving, because supplies need to be constantly replenished for future collectors, which is exactly what Retro is doing.

Retro is a good illustration of how one's age can affect the interpretation of "old." To the computer generation born in the 1970s, Elvis seems as outdated as 1930s film goddess Greta Garbo does to baby boomers. Retro pieces are to me what 1920s furniture was to my grandmother. When I was a teen collector showing Gram what I considered a treasure, she exclaimed, "Why do you want that? I threw one out just like it forty years ago."

Now in this new century, I refuse to say anything like that to my nephew Ryan. When he shows Uncle Frank what I consider a less-

Here is the number one Mid Century piece: a lounge chair and an ottoman designed by Charles and Ray Eames and made by Herman Miller in the 1950s and 1960s.

Treadway Toomey Galleries

than-ancient memento, I reply with a chuckle, "Retro is awesome." As for the question, "Is it junk or antique?," I leave that answer to you. Just collect what pleases you.

You are on your way to becoming fluent in antiquese. The next chapter begins your learning adventure.

Chapter 2

How Antiques Embellish Our Lives

Now that you have mastered the definition of antiques and semi-antiques/collectibles, I want to demonstrate how antiques embellish our lives. There are so many fabulous ways that I want to make sure you become familiar with all of them.

The best means of revealing the magic of antiques is by presenting a tale of someone who really missed the antiques boat. Once there was a ruler who rarely if ever smiled, and here is the cause of his gloom. Legend records an account of this sovereign who erred royally when he turned down an opportunity to acquire a magnificent piece of French furniture. If this infamous noncollector found out who now possesses this crème de la crème antique, he would turn over in his regal tomb.

At the height of his power, Napoleon I, Emperor of France from 1804 to 1815, was offered an elegant cabinet that formerly belonged to in-laws of martyred Queen Marie Antoinette of France. The war-loving Bonaparte, lacking appreciation for curios, snootily replied, "His majesty wants the new and not to buy old." What benefits do antiques offer that Napoleon so carelessly overlooked? The perks fall into four groups: practical, financial, intellectual and emotional.

Practical Perks

MOTHER NATURE LOVES ANTIQUES

One of the oldest forms of recycling is collecting, which of course benefits nature. Reusing antiques decreases the amount of rubbish entering garbage dumps. And many trees continue to thrive, thanks to antique furniture reducing the demand for fresh timber.

A 1940s Pepsi radio reminds us of the "Pepsi Generation," or "baby boomers" in today's jargon.

Forsythes' Auctions

Skinner Auctions, Inc.

What patriotism is strirred by this early 1800s needlepoint and watercolor of Mount Vernon!

No Assembly Required

A while back, I wanted to become more high tech, so I bought a new computer desk for my office. (At the time an antique model seemed impractical for this purpose.) I gave up a postcard-perfect fall weekend to put the desk together and ended up with damaged pride and scratched knuckles to boot. Unlike most new furniture, or practically anything else for our homes, antiques don't require assembly. If you're like your antiques coach, who is mechanically handicapped, this is one grand benefit.

Financial Perks

Antiques Give More Dash for Your Cash

Last year at an outdoor show in Allegan, Michigan, a reddish vintage 1910 mahogany sheet music cabinet won my favor. It ended up in my new office and cost only $90. This 4-foot high, 20-inch wide cabinet has interior shelves perfect for storing toner and copier paper.

How extraordinary that in the 21st century a reddish mahogany cabinet almost 100 years old could be purchased for $90! But it's true. Although this piece isn't museum caliber, it is well made and adds charm to my office. In contrast, what can you buy new for $90 even at Target? You can actually stretch your budget while getting better quality preassembled furniture by shopping for antiques.

ANTIQUES RETAIN VALUE BETTER THAN NEW

The instant a new item leaves a store, it's considered used merchandise and, therefore, plummets in value. Have you been to a garage sale where a downtrodden soul was trying to peddle a six-month old sofa? That demoralized individual might have been your antiques coach. After a day of wheeling and dealing on my driveway, I was thrilled to get $65 for that $650 couch. That experience taught me that antiques are far better investments compared to new items.

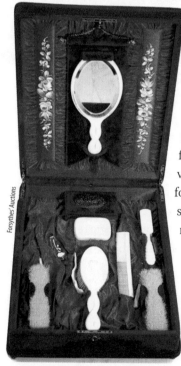

Forsythes' Auctions

Milady's dresser set from the late 1800s is an example of how clever people were in the old days. Its case had a music box.

ANTIQUES MAY INCREASE IN VALUE

Unlike my former sofa, antiques usually maintain their value and even appreciate. If you compare past prices to current, you'll be startled to see how much they've swelled. For instance, when I was a graduate student on an exchange program in Paris, I bought a very ornate 1860s French clock for the then princely sum of $25. Today, a similar version complete with a figurine could easily sell for $350 to $450 at auction. Best of all, looking ever-so-Parisian on the mantel, it still thrills me, evoking memories of the City of Light.

ANTIQUES OFFER HIGHER QUALITY

It's a cinch to verify that antiques are usually better made than modern counterparts. Older houses, as you know, have plastered walls, while contemporary homes use drywall. A similar disparity in quality exists between antiques and new goods. Contemporary furniture routinely has particleboard or cardboard backs, unlike solid wood backs used in antiques. Modern "carving" on pieces is usually plastic, not painstakingly hand carved detailing so prevalent in vintage pieces. Another drawback is that new furniture is assembled with weak, garish staples, and usually lacks glue and screws. The same contrast in quality is evident in other products, from china to silver. While some modern goods are well made, they are rare and very expensive. How many of us have checkbooks that can tackle their lofty prices?

This early 1900s Swiss musical Christmas tree stand shows us how inventive our not-too-distant ancestors were.

Remember my tale of scraped knuckles and a lost weekend spent assembling that computer desk? That piece of junk fell apart two years later. Guess what type of desk I now have in my new office? That's right, a good old mahogany model complete with glue, screws and solid brass handles.

Intellectual Perks
ANTIQUES TEACH HISTORY

Antiques make great history instructors, thanks to the personal and interesting insights they offer into past lifestyles. For example, have you ever wondered why most old beds are undersized compared to contemporary examples? Of course our ancestors were generally shorter, but there is another reason. People rarely slept as we do, but rather in a semireclined position, propped up by many pillows. To sleep fully horizontal was considered unhealthy because it was feared that blood rushing to the head could cause death.

Emotional Perks
ANTIQUES PROVIDE MINI VACATIONS

Movies starring Fred Astaire and Ginger Rogers temporarily relieved the hardships of the Depression for 1930s audiences. Antiquing can also relieve stress and fatigue. For example, even though I got up at 3 a.m. to catch my flight home following the Atlantiques City Show, I made plans to go antiquing that same morning with my friends. Soon after arriving in Cincin-

This cuckoo clock from the Black Forest of Germany, possibly a souvenir, recalls a pleasant holiday there.

nati, I met Denny and Anne, and by 9 a.m., we were were rummaging through lane after lane at the Burlington Antiques Market. I felt truly energized. Only after arriving home did fatigue set in. That's the joy of antiquing: stress and fatigue are temporarily forgotten as you check everything out. (One word of advice: frequently say to yourself, "Just because I'm antiquing doesn't mean I have to buy something".)

ANTIQUES PROMOTE BONDING

Another benefit of antiquing is that it creates lifelong friendships. I often fondly reminisce with my buddies Pete and Dianne about one of our best-ever antiques rendezvous in the French paradise known as the Parisian Flea Market. We have grown to respect our different tastes and shopping styles. At shows, one of us is the meanderer while the other two are sprinters. Our diverse modes complement each other; Dianne has spotted gems that we too-hurried guys missed.

Antiques can work the same magic with relatives and, yes, even with siblings. Antiquing has made my sister and me even better chums, and we often plan our summer get-togethers around outdoor shows and visits to nearby antiques shops. Her husband, Ron, and their son, Ryan, sometimes join us. We someday hope to snag my niece, "Miss" Mackenzie, and her husband, Kris, into our collecting group.

ANTIQUES AND FENG SHUI

For centuries the Chinese have followed Feng Shui, the art of arranging objects to promote positive energy in surroundings. The philosophy incorporates many principles, but one in particular especially pertains to antiques.

One of the tenets of Feng Shui is the importance of surrounding ourselves with possessions

Forsythes' Auctions

No doubt this "Modernola" round phonograph with lamp circa 1910 has seen some cheerful occasions.

Ted Williams' Red Sox uniform from 1959 evokes the joy of watching baseball.

that bring happiness and harmony. Antiques do this better than practically anything else. One experience in particular touched me forever. While I was helping with the *Antiques Roadshow* in Louisville, Kentucky, a lady vigilantly holding a pink and white French teacup and saucer really brought home the meaning of Feng Shui. It wasn't easy for her to hold her treasure, for her hands were deformed. But her grin reflected her rapture as she chattered about her grandmother's china. Just sharing her joy with me seemed to erase any embarrassment or discomfort. (I truly hoped that she would receive a kind and favorable appraisal.)

A glance at a beloved heirloom can give you a thrill. Precious family mementos keep beloved relatives always in your heart and give you peaceful thoughts during rough times. Just looking at my ruby glass pitcher from the Chicago's World Fair of 1893 reminds me how Gram gave me my first-ever antique. Antiques will lift your spirits and constantly comfort you. They did for the lady at the *Antiques Roadshow*, whom I call "my Louisville hero," and they will do it for you, too.

ANTIQUES AND PETS ARE THE INTERNATIONAL LANGUAGE OF FRIENDSHIP

Have you ever been at a tedious gathering full of bragging, yawns, clock watching, hot political debates and trivial jabber? Then, miraculously, the room becomes blissfully noisy, full of giggling and happy banter. Why? Someone probably mentioned pets. Conversations about antiques create that same magic. Strangers have become buddies comparing shows, dealers, prices and collections. Dogs, cats and antiques bring out the best in people and are part of the international language of friendship.

This painting of three children dating from 1835 must bring its lucky owner much joy.

Skinner Auctions, Inc.

Now back to the sad Emperor. Do you know why few (if any) portraits of Napoleon show him smiling? By vetoing that regal cabinet, the Emperor really missed out on a masterpiece. And, as you now realize, his life was never embellished by the bonuses that come with antiques. To add salt to the wound, a descendent of his archenemy, King George III, now owns this stellar antique. According to David Linley in *Extraordinary Furniture*, Queen Elizabeth II has the pleasure of looking at this incredible beauty in her private apartments at Windsor Castle.

Forsythes' Auctions

This papier-mâché Nipper for RCA Victor testifies that antiques and dogs go hand-in-hand.

Chapter 3

No More French, S'il Vous Plait!

You're now ready for the next phase in your *Antiques 101* adventure. We're going to explore more terms dealing with antiques, but we'll avoid many unnecessary hurdles by eliminating most difficult French names (a few exceptions mentioned later are justified).

Why avoid French? After all, it's a charming language with a romantic reputation. And it's true that "Rue de la Paix" sounds more refined and elegant than "Peace Street." But have you ever been in the middle of a novel sprinkled with French phrases and been stumped at a critical point in the plot? Whether the author used French to establish a certain atmosphere or merely to impress, you're left perplexed and frustrated.

Loomism

Avoid French terms to describe antiques.

Garth's Auctions, Inc.

How many of us know that a bureau plat refers to a desk?

Jackson's International Auctions

Unfortunately, French is used extensively in beautiful but impractical coffee table books about antiques. You know the type: the prominently displayed glossy volumes intended to proclaim their owners' sophistication. But does anyone actually read these books? Why slog through difficult passages when English is easier and clearer? For instance, the English term "antique calling cards" is more straightforward (although admittedly less dignified) than the French name "cartes de visites." Although small cases used as manicure or sewing sets are fun to acquire, most people outside France would not know what an "etui" is.

Say "desk" instead of "escritoire" if you wish to be understood by most Yankees.

What is a "boutinierre"? Sounds like something a gentleman wears when he gets married, but it is actually a cupboard.

Du Mouchelle's Auction

Forsythes' Auctions

The English word "chair" comes from the French word "chaise."

Victorians loved to sprinkle French expressions in daily conversations. This was considered the height of refinement because France at that time was the artistic hub of the universe, but the practice often created confusion. Pie served with ice cream was called "pie ala mode," but the phrase literally means "stylish pie." Similarly, "pomme frites" should actually be called "deep fried potatoes" rather than "French fries." (Incidentally, "French" fries were first made in Belgium.) And if you call a chest of drawers by its French name, "commode," you might raise some eyebrows, because in America "commode" means toilet.

So let's leave French for the French. Do practice French expressions when dining in a French restaurant or vacationing in that splendid county. However, when discussing antiques on this side of the Atlantic, let's use English.

In Paris, the word "canapé" means sofa, but it is pronounced like "can of ..." well, you get the idea.

Garth's Auctions, Inc.

Forsythes' Auctions

On the western side of the Atlantic, calling these nightstands "commodes" might be embarrassing.

Jackson's International Auctions

In French, "etageres" means "stairs," but Victorians loved to use this term for whatnot shelves.

Chapter 4

What's Your Antiques Personality?

Have you ever wondered what type of antiques personality you have? Collectors tend to follow two diverse decorating paths. The Georgian favors the understated 1700s styles. The two "C" trademarks of the Victorian era, clutter and curlicue, ruled during the mid- to late-1800s. Neither taste is better than the other. As I often point out in my classes, "Good taste is in the eye of the antiquer," so don't let self-appointed decorating gurus sway your collecting preferences. Collect what makes you smile.

Loomism

Collectors tend to follow two diverse decorating paths: Georgian or Victorian.

A Pop Quiz

To determine your antiques personality, answer the following questions:

For china, which of the following do you prefer?

a. An all-white service with just one small central floral motif

b. An overall floral motif of many colors with a thick gold band

For side chairs?

a. One with little, if any, carving

b. A model with carved curlicues and gold trim

How many photos do you like to have on the table next to your favorite chair or sofa?

a. One is plenty, thank you!

b. The more the merrier!

If you like simple china patterns, unadorned chairs and a single photo per table, chances are you favor the more organized, understated tastes prevalent in the 1700s. On the other hand, if you think the more gold and flowers on your china the better, or curlicues and myriad pictures make you happy, then you're a Victorian type of collector.

Both Georgian and Victorian styles are named after British monarchs who ruled when these two contrasting tastes were (for the first time) very popular.

The Georgian Mantel
The Georgian style is named after the four King George Hanovers who ruled England from 1714 to 1830. Georgian furniture, silver, china and other household items were crafted

If the understated look of this fine grandfather clock, possibly made by Herschede of Cincinnati, circa 1910, whets your antiques whistle, you probably prefer less ornate antiques.

Jackson's International Auctions

Forsythes' Auctions

If the ornateness of this Symphonion grandfather clock with music box stirs you, you just may have a Victorian collecting spirit.

in assorted styles, but compared to the furnishings of the succeeding era, most 1700s pieces seem rather staid.

As Georgian understatement ruled in Britain and America, furniture was sparse and low-key, lacking ostentatious touches such as gilt decoration. A Georgian mantel generally held a pair of vases, one on each side of a centrally placed bowl, and a single picture was centered above the fireplace.

The Victorian Mantel

The Victorian period was named for Queen Victoria, who ruled Great Britain after the death of the last male Hanover, William IV. Thus, home furnishings made during her long reign from 1837 to 1901 have become known as "Victorian."

Around the time President and Mrs. Abraham Lincoln moved into the White House, decorating tastes changed dramatically. Most goods for homes, whether chairs or teapots, were being machine-made rather than produced by hand, which was a much slower and more expensive process. By the 1870s, prosperity bloomed, and the number of middle-class households rose dramatically. Such abundance, plus more affordable and plentiful furnishings, increased clutter.

Forsythes' Auctions

Here's another lavish chair from the Victorian era.

Forsythes' Auctions

This may look like a chair, but it is actually a harp stand. How Victorians loved pomposity!

During this period, Victorians crammed as many lace doilies, vases, photos and candlesticks onto their mantels as could possibly fit. In addition, numerous smaller pictures flanked the central one hung on the wall without concern for balance.

A Final Option: The Eclectic Style

The choice is yours: Georgian or Victorian. But if you don't find either of these styles completely satisfying, and you answered the quiz with both a's and b's, then you're like me and prefer eclectic collecting, which combines both Georgian and Victorian tastes. Lucky us—our tastes reveal a Renaissance spirit. Rather than limiting our collecting to one era or style, this alternative offers many more wonderful antiques.

No matter what your antiques personality, most collectors love vintage Christmas antiques. This Christmas tree has a key-wound musical stand.

Forsythes' Auctions

Chapter 5
A Tale of Two Antiques Cities

Throughout history, many countries, including China, Japan, Italy, Holland, as well as those in Scandinavia and Africa, have created magnificent antiques. But to learn antiques styles in the most efficient way possible, we'll focus on France, Great Britain and the United States.

For centuries, a rather tenuous relationship existed between England and France. The relationship between the two countries flanking the narrow English Channel got off to a rather rocky start when the Frenchman William the Conqueror (1027-1087) defeated England. History reveals that William won the battle of Hastings in 1066 and became the king of England. Sadly, as a result of that struggle, the two nations remained enemies for centuries and

George Washington embellishes this circa 1810 Parisian clock made by Dubuc.

Skinner Auctions, Inc.

fought many wars. However, continual struggles never stopped the movement of designs in clothing, art, food and furnishings from Paris to London.

Charles Dickens best described Paris and London by titling his epic novel *A Tale of Two Cities*. The French often borrowed or sometimes reinterpreted a design from other countries. The British would then copy the French version, but usually less ornately. Then, beginning in the mid-1700s, "Yankee" interpretations appeared that closely imitated the French.

Today, England and France are finally allies, as illustrated by the construction of the "Chunnel" under the English Channel, allowing trains to travel between the two cities in just a few hours. We owe this relationship, which always existed artistically, but rarely politically, to three great political figures: Great Britain's Queen Victoria and France's Napoleon III and his wife Eugénie. These rulers initi-

Jackson's International Auctions

American collectors love Parisian scenes like this early 20th century example by French artist Edouard Leon Cortes (1882-1969).

ated their "good neighbor" policy when they governed their respective countries. Later when we examine Rococo Revival, we will also discover how influential they were on home décor.

In the early 20th century, the New York firm Slack Rassnick & Company created this chest in an interpretation of the French Louis XVI style.

Garth's Auctions, Inc.

Chapter 6
All About Woods

As you scan these photos for the first time, you will notice various furniture styles mentioned. Don't get bogged down. After you finish this primer, go back and look at these pictures again and again. They will help you master the woods and styles.

Perhaps it never occurred to you that antique furniture originally came from living trees. That concept never came to my mind either until I started teaching. One day a student asked, "What kind of tree grows mahogany?" I stumbled for an answer because I had always thought of wood as the nonliving material used to make a chair or table rather than as the living substance that forms a growing tree. After a few nerve-wracking moments, the obvious dawned on me. "A mahogany tree grows mahogany," I finally announced with much relief. My student's excellent question illustrates the importance of recognizing woods. Being familiar with the principal timbers used to craft antique furniture will help make learning antiques styles a breeze.

Kudos for Veneer

When Denny, Anne and I ventured to the Burlington Antiques Market that I told you about in Chapter 2, I immediately put my detective skills into action. As Anne and I were looking for a coffee table for her mother, my ears perked up at a comment I overheard. Two shoppers were flirting with a 1850s chest of drawers. The dealer graciously announced to one of them, "I can do better on price," but she declined the offer with the comment, "It's veneer and not real wood."

Somehow veneer has become synonymous with shoddy quality, which is absolutely incorrect. Just as yellow

Forsythes' Auctions

This Empire Revival sheet music cabinet with claw feet features inlay, or marquetry, on its door.

icing suggests that a cake is yellow inside and out, veneer creates the same impression with furniture. Veneering takes much skill to glue a very thin layer of expensive wood over a less costly piece. Veneer is a mark of craftsmanship, one that keeps prices in line by using rare woods sparingly.

The Big Six

The six main woods used for antique furniture can be divided into three easy-to-remember groups: two auburns (mahogany and cherry), one brunette (walnut), and three blonds (oak, maple and pine).

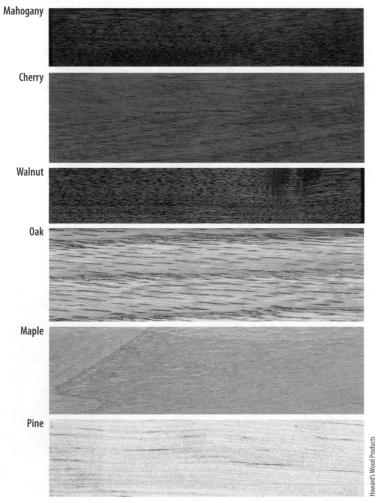

The samples above show the grains and colors of popular woods.

The Auburns

MAHOGANY

Mahogany has traditionally been associated with urban furniture rather than country pieces. Its rather staid grain is the color of cordovan leather or rosé wine. Imported from the West Indies and Central America, it was customarily used for upscale furniture. By 1750, it had become the wood of choice for aristocratic homes in London, New York, Boston and Charleston, and was used for drawing room or dining room pieces. Several major furniture styles chiefly used mahogany. Thomas Chippendale, a legendary cabinetmaker from the 1700s, was celebrated for his mahogany masterpieces. Mahogany's strength made it possible for this incomparable artisan to carve ball-and-claw feet in minute detail.

During the 1890s, mahogany was again very popular and was often used for music cabinets like this beautiful model with cabriole legs.

CHERRY

If anyone were to ask what your favorite wood is, I'd bet that, like most collectors, cherry tops your list. Cherry grew almost everywhere in the United States, making it a natural for rural pieces. Cherry resembles mahogany but with a slightly paler color—more like a blush wine. Cherry provided the strength country folks needed for durable furnishings. But these days, it's easy to forget cherry's humble origin because it gives mahogany a run for big antiques bucks.

Cherry features another sensational trait. Within its pinkish grain are champagne-colored veins resembling streaks of lightning. This lively mixture of rose and off-white adds just the right amount of zing to rural pieces, which often were rather plain compared to city furniture.

Mahogany made this cabinet with its Aesthetic Movement carving on its door an upscale piece when brand new in the 1890s.

Forsythes' Auctions

The Globe Wernicke firm of Cincinnati crafted sectional/stack/barrister bookcases from mahogany, as well as oak.

NEAR TWINS

Savvy cabinetmakers in the early 1800s often put mahogany and cherry on the same piece. Solid cherry was incorporated on the sides, while costlier mahogany veneers were used on drawer fronts. Thus, mahogany veneer and cherry, so similar in color, made chests of drawers appear totally made from mahogany. Such strategies helped cherry become known as "the poor man's mahogany" and is another testimony to the value of veneer.

The Lone Brunette
WALNUT

Walnut, the only brunette of "The Big Six," is universally loved and grows the world over. Like chocolate fudge, walnut comes in a wide range of hues from light to dark. Walnut's porous grain makes it very durable. Before 1720, walnut was the premier choice for European and American furniture. Its heyday marked one of the most beautiful styles of furniture ever crafted, the Queen Anne style. Rural American country pieces such as cupboards and benches were routinely made from walnut.

Why has walnut remained venerated while the demand for other woods comes and goes? Its enduring popularity is to due to what I call its "blue blazer" quality. As any clothes horse can testify, blue blazers aren't on the cutting edge of fashion, but they're practical and timeless. Like the blue blazer, walnut works well in any style or era.

The Blonds
OAK

The most well-known blond is oak, which grows in Europe and the United States. English oak tends to be darker than American because of climactic differences. Its durability made it a natural choice for the construction of houses and ships, as well as furniture. In fact, before the 1700s, oak was one of the chief woods for British and European furniture. Of all the woods, oak is the easiest to spot. Just rub your fingers along a piece to feel its lively grain. Like most blonds, oak comes in various shades from Chablis to beer.

GOLDEN OAK
"Golden Oak" refers to American furniture made around 1900. The classic round dining tables with carved, hairy animal claw feet were usually made from golden oak. As the finish aged, a lovely, deep amber color emerged, giving birth to its charming name.

Oak was a favorite for stack/sectional/barrister bookcases made by Globe Wernicke of Cincinnati. Each glass-faced section was a totally self-contained component and was a forerunner of modern sectional furniture.

In the late 1800s and early 1900s, oak china closets were considered the height of chic.

This ornate hall seat in the Renaissance Revival style was crafted from oak around 1890.

Forsythes' Auctions

Who wouldn't want to own this incredible oak bookcase that originally graced a Victorian library?

Forsythes' Auctions

MAPLE

Maple trees grow across the globe, and of course, could any one imagine pancakes without the sweet syrup from Vermont maples? Maple ranges in color from off-white to an apple cider tone. At first, you may find it difficult to spot its fine grain, but in no time at all you'll be able to distinguish its slight veining. Give a maple cutting board a good rap with your knuckles and you'll feel its strength and solidity. This explains why this blond wood was used mainly for rural pieces and was rarely carved. Maple remains an excellent choice for chair legs and cutting boards because of its great durability.

Skinner Auctions, Inc.

This bookcase from around 1825 was painted to capture the look of tiger-striped maple. Of all the woods, maple is the most joyful.

A Blond Veneer

Bird's-eye veneer earned its name from the swirling designs created by the knots in maple trees. Cabinetmakers dressed up plain-looking walnut and cherry chests of drawers by gluing thin bird's-eye maple panels to drawer fronts. This process, while requiring expertise, was easier than carving decorations, which not only took great skill, but much time and perspiration.

The Last Blond: The Christmas Wood

Every December, many of us decorate pine trees, blonds common to Europe and North America. Become familiar with this wood by surveying its very pale and vibrant graining. Once considered low end—the spaghetti of timber—pine is now in vogue. In the past, pine was veneered, painted or hidden on the back and inside of furniture. Even George Washington had his pine walls in Mount Vernon grain-painted to make the foyer appear paneled in swankier mahogany. Now, pine, like spaghetti, has gained prestige. Just as spaghetti is no longer relegated to blue-plate specials but is served as a trendy dish at fashionable Italian restaurants, pine has similarly risen in status.

Pine's current popularity is in no small part due to its neutral color, which goes so well with furniture crafted from other woods. Gram pointed out another perk coming from pine's light coloring. Unlike darker woods such as mahogany or walnut, pine hides dust better, reducing housework.

This beautiful pine cupboard made in Virginia dates from the mid-1800s.

Garth's Auctions, Inc.

Staining and Varnishing

A few words about stain and varnish will enhance your knowledge about furniture. Stain is a weak colored solution applied to duplicate the shade of another wood. Cabinetmakers commonly used stain to make furniture look as if made entirely from a single type of wood rather than several.

Rarely did this process look totally natural. Mahogany stain emerged iodine-red. Maple, all the rage during the Early American craze of the 1950s (like the furnishings in the Ricardo's Connecticut house in *I Love Lucy*) tended to develop an iridescent orange tone. Cherry became garish pink, while oak became far too dark. Only walnut, the blue-blazer wood, escaped this fate.

While staining changed colors, it offered no preservation, necessitating a protective coat of varnish. The varnish, a solution of resins of alcohol or linseed oil, was applied on stained or unstained surfaces to create a transparent but impenetrable coat, much the same way glass protects a framed print.

It is sometimes hard to distinguish woods because of stains that have been applied. This pine cupboard, dating from the American Revolution, has red stain that was probably used to try to duplicate the hue of mahogany or cherry.

Skinner Auctions, Inc.

Touring Lumberyards

To master the various types of raw (unstained) timbers, visit lumber-yards. And while your fingers are exploring the grains and textures, enjoy the intoxicating aroma of fresh lumber. The smell of cut wood is as pleasurable as freshly mowed grass and sun-dried laundry. Be sure to make mental notes of your sensory impressions, as they will greatly enhance your furniture training.

Get a good look at the lively oak graining on this dining table that is a mixture of Empire Revival (claw feet) and Renaissance Revival (griffin legs). The choice veneer on the apron is known as quarter-sawn oak because of the way it was cut to show off as much graining as possible.

Visiting Stores, Shows and Museums

Go antiquing to find furniture pieces made of the "The Big Six" woods. Stay alert and pay careful attention to the accompanying descriptions. These are learning opportunities to be savored. Closely examine and caress various woods to learn their color, grain and feel. You'll be surprised at how distinctive each wood actually is.

Exploring Museums

While it's necessary for museums to keep their masterpieces out of reach, it's frustrating for those of us who want to touch. But even

The stellar inlays on this desk
make it obvious why the
Dutch have been celebrated
for their marquetry.

Forsythes' Auctions

though their treasures can't be caressed, a
museum's superb displays and descriptions
provide unparalleled opportunities for learning. Read—look at objects—scan descriptions again—take final looks—but be sure
to avoid the alarms! In just a few hours at a
museum, you can absorb a great deal of useful information.

Empire Revival pieces such as this china
closet were often crafted from oak.

Forsythes' Auctions

SECTION TWO

Antiques Styles

Chapter 7

Queen Anne: Understated Elegance

Our first great furniture style dates from the days of Queen Anne of England, who ruled from 1702 to 1714. This monarch's greatest accomplishment was the unification of Scotland and England into Great Britain. During her reign, another magical transformation also occurred. Colossal furniture so prevalent in earlier times with protruding, ghostly carvings was swept away in favor of more lightweight designs. This style, named "Queen Anne" in her honor, has earned the monarch more fame than other rulers who have built grand palaces or won great battles.

What better starting place for our furniture study! The Queen Anne style is not a mere trend but a timeless standard for grace and

Three prime examples of the Queen Anne style, all dating from the mid-1700s: a drop leaf table, a candlestick stand and a side chair.

beauty. While other antique styles come and go, Queen Anne remains the star. Yes, this is my favorite, but countless antiquers and museum curators wholeheartedly agree. I like to call Queen Anne style the "Katharine Hepburn" of antiques. As other movie actresses emerged and then disappeared in the 20th century, Miss Hepburn, a leading lady in films for 60 years, collected four Oscars and will always be acclaimed. Likewise, the Queen Anne style is the eternal antique luminary—always adaptable, fashionable, timeless and universally adored.

Queen Anne Trademarks

COMFORT AND MODERN DESIGN

Are you wondering how a 300-year-old style could possibly qualify as comfortable and even modern? During Queen Anne's reign, an ingenious cabinetmaker invented modern furniture. Previously, chair backs were rigidly perpendicular to seats. Comfort finally arrived with the introduction of a back that followed the spine's curve. This revolutionary model, known as the spoon back, has a central wooden backrest shaped like a vase or fiddle.

Many 1700s cabinetmakers, besides being decorators, operated as informal confidents for female clients. Perhaps a duchess complained: "Well, those new chair backs are divine, my dear, but what about those paltry seats?" Along with spoon backs, progress in the comfort department materialized again when a responsive craftsman widened the standard tiny seat into a more commodious horseshoe shape. How wholeheartedly welcomed this enhancement must have been in the days of hoop skirts. Sitting on a Queen Anne chair, our backs and posteriors are certainly grateful for those two features.

THE CABRIOLE LEG

"Cabriole" legs, the primary trait of Queen Anne, make identifying this style a snap. In Chapter 3, I recommended avoiding most French terms, but I said a few exceptions are justified. "Cabriole" is one of those exceptions. It's one French term too splendid to toss aside. The supposedly equivalent English term, "goat" or "bow" leg, leaves much to be desired, don't you think? In this case, the French justly win the contest of English versus French terminology.

The rounded cabriole leg repeats the curvy look so prevalent on

Feast your eyes on the cabriole legs of this cherry Connecticut tea table from the late 1700s.

Skinner Auctions, Inc.

A walnut Queen Anne lowboy, or dressing table, from Pennsylvania dating from 1730 to 1760. Notice its pad feet.

Skinner Auctions, Inc.

This maple dressing table, circa 1740, has the definitive cabriole legs terminating in pad feet.

Skinner Auctions, Inc.

spoon back chairs. The technical description of cabriole leg is a knee leg with concave (rounded) ankle. The leg ends in a duck or pad-shaped foot. You can find the same curvy shape on an apron, (the horizontal front piece located just under the seat between chair legs), and on single or double curved fronts on chests of drawers.

The English borrowed cabriole legs from the French and Dutch, who pilfered the design from Spain. In the late 1600s, as the French became enraptured with the design, they adopted the word "cabriole" from the Spanish word "capra." At about the same time, the Dutch began crafting cabriole legs for furniture. When William and his wife Mary (Queen Anne's older sister) left the Netherlands to become King and Queen of England, furniture with cabriole legs were no doubt part of the royal possessions.

LACK OF CARVING

Sparse carving is another halllmark that will help you recognize the Queen Anne style. Aversion to ornateness was an artistic reaction against earlier Frankensteinish furniture. The minimal carving creates a soothing, uncluttered feeling that has kept the Queen Anne style contemporary for three centuries.

USE OF WALNUT

The Queen Anne cabinetmaker had other tricks in his tool box to make designs appealing. For example, lighter-hued walnut replaced somber oak as the most fashionable wood. While not flamboyant, walnut is always adaptable and serviceable, like blue blazers.

A very early English Queen Anne chest of drawers, circa 1720, has glorious walnut veneer.

Later Queen Anne Trademarks

THE SECOND QUEEN ANNE LEG

Before the 1720s, horizontal wooden braces called stretchers were often placed between delicate cabriole legs for extra reinforcement. But by the late 1720s and 1730s, cabriole legs grew stouter and stronger, making stretchers unnecessary. Usually, front legs were cabriole-shaped, while the rear two were straight to provide added strength. Many country Queen Anne pieces have rounded, straight legs that are hardly cabriole, but are quite handsome nonetheless. Country cabinetmakers didn't know how to make the complicated cabriole leg, so the rural version was turned on a lathe. These pieces are still charming and are emblazoned with other Queen Anne traits like shell carving.

BALL-AND-CLAW FEET

Early Queen Anne chairs had thin cabriole legs and simple pad or duck feet. But when England started trading in the Canton region of China in 1635, the British became crazy for Chinese products like silk, tea, and blue and white porcelain. A cabinetmaker who wanted to cash in on the frenzy tried to increase furniture sales by copying the Chinese ball-and-claw foot. According to Chinese mythology, this design symbolized a dragon's paw holding the pearl of wisdom. In the next chapter, we'll learn about a cabinetmaker who carried this motif to perfection.

SHELL CARVING

The success of the ball-and-claw feet set off a yearning to add a little dash to conservative Queen Anne furniture. The carved rounded shell added decoration without becoming excessive. This symbol had been the emblem of the Crusaders who fought the Moslems to free the Holy Land. During the early days of King Louis XV, this motif emerged at Versailles, the fabled chateau near Paris. London, ever conscious of Parisian trends, very cautiously added Rococo shells to the knees of cabriole legs, chair aprons, drawer fronts and the top wooden splat

Loomism

Queen Anne has two substyles: (1) Early Queen Anne lacks carving and has simple duck or pad feet and thin cabriole legs. (2) Later Queen Anne features the ball-and-claw foot, thicker cabriole legs and a modest amount of carving, typically of shells.

(horizontal bar) of chair backs. Such embellishments, added ever so sparingly, still kept the Queen Anne style understated compared to previous designs. No one wanted to return to the gloomy garish furniture of past generations.

Queen Anne Stars

One way to keep the Queen Anne style etched in your mind is to remember the following three definitive examples.

HOGARTH CHAIRS

The British artist William Hogarth (1697-1764), who was known for engravings that spoofed British society, praised cabriole legs. The artist wrote in *The Analysis of Beauty* (1753), that "the cabriole leg...is adding grace to beauty." Soon "fiddle backs" became known as "Hogarth" chairs. This is just one of many examples of chairs being named after famous people.

HIGHBOYS

Highboys are to Queen Anne what the Eiffel Tower is to Paris. Just as Paris would not be the same city without its grandest tourist attraction, one could not imagine this style without highboys. In the late 1600s, highboys were first created in England and were known as tall boys, and by the mid-1700s, Colonial cabinet makers created superb highboys.

The highboy consists of a chest of drawers resting upon a base that held one to three drawers. All this stylishness was supported by magnificent cabriole legs. Earliest examples had flat tops, while later versions came with broken arch pediments

A gorgeous Queen Anne cherry-and-maple scroll-top highboy, also known as a high chest of drawers, circa 1760 to 1780.

Skinner Auctions, Inc.

Jackson's International Auctions

**This flat top English Queen Anne highboy in
burl walnut dates from the early 1700s.**

complete with finials. This stylish decoration resembled a triangular
piece of wood with a cut-out center. Finials were wooden urn-shaped
ornaments, a motif borrowed from ancient times. Tall case or grandfather clocks had similar pediment tops, but finials were usually metal
such as brass.

Skinner Auctions, Inc.

This Queen Anne high chest of drawers/highboy was hand painted in an oriental motif known as japanning and dates from 1735 to 1739. Notice its cabriole legs and deeply carved oval-shaped feet on pads.

By the late 1700s, the Brits switched to chests on chests, which are literally one chest of drawers resting upon a lower one. Thankfully, Yankee craftsmen, having perfected highboy designs, made these crème-de-la-crème antiques as late as 1800.

LOWBOYS
The lowboy is another definitive Queen Anne antique. "Lowboy" is a more recent nickname for dressing or toilet table (or vanity), which in the 1700s held milady's beauty paraphernalia. Dressing tables were often matching pieces for highboys. Resembling a small highboy base, lowboys usually had three small drawers, and occasionally a long fourth one above the lower three.

AN ERA ENDS BUT A STYLE ENDURES
The Queen Anne style continued to be crafted in both Britain and America long after Queen Anne died. Keep in mind that there is never a stop date when one style ends and a brand new one abruptly takes over. Most designs slide into each other, meaning the old was still being crafted as the latest was becoming fashionable. In the following section, you will encounter one of the all-time great furniture styles, which in many ways is based on Queen Anne trademarks.

Skinner Auctions, Inc.

Keep this cherry dressing table from the 1750s in mind as a definitive example of the Queen Anne style.

Chapter 8

Chippendale: The King of Mahogany

After Queen Anne's death, an international search for a Protestant relative was begun to keep Great Britain Anglican rather than having the nation return to Roman Catholicism. A distant family member named Sophia was tracked down in Hanover, a Prussian province in northwestern Germany. In 1714, Sophia's son, the head of the Hanover dynasty, was crowned George I. The succeeding monarch became George II (1683-1760), the grandfather of colonial America's final King, George III (1738-1820). The last of the Georges during the 1800s, George IV (1762-1830), was quite a connoisseur of fine wine, food, furnishings and mademoiselles. The combined reigns of these four kings is called the Georgian Era.

In England and Europe, furniture made before the Georgian Era was rarely named for the artist who designed it, but rather after the reigning monarch. Thus, English furniture with cabriole legs became known as Queen Anne style. Use monarch names for styles that date before 1750, but for more recent designs, that rule changes, as you are about to discover.

An upholstered Chippendale sofa is remarkably comfortable.

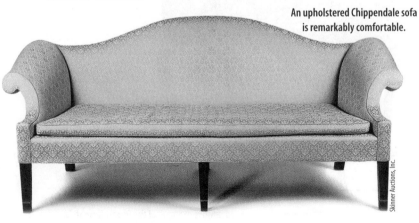

Skinner Auctions, Inc.

The Post Queen Anne/Early Georgian Era

The Queen Anne style remained popular during the reigns of George I and George II. Changes in personal tastes, whether in bonnets or chairs, occurred slowly in the 1700s. Keeping pace with fashion was not nearly as enslaving then as today because our "throw away" mentality didn't exist at that time. And since handmade replacements were costly and required long waits, most damaged possessions were not cast off; socks were darned, and broken furnishings were fixed. Similarly, furniture wasn't demoted to attics or cellars when no longer stylish. Perhaps an aging Queen Anne side chair was occasionally relegated to a guest room when a trendier model arrived for the drawing room, but only rarely.

Just two decades before the American Revolution, innovative furniture ushered a breakthrough in interior decoration. As you learned in the previous chapter, a more robust Queen Anne style with carving and stouter cabriole legs was introduced to London, and a short time later, in America as well. In addition, mahogany imported from the New World replaced walnut and oak as the premier wood.

The Age of Mahogany

"The Age of Mahogany" marked the end of oak and walnut as the leading woods for stylish furnishings. Mahogany's glory years, 1720 to 1860, included four spectacular furniture styles that will soon become second nature to you. The bluestocking set chose rosé-hued pieces for salons (a good French word fashionable in Britain and America, which in the 1800s was replaced by the term "parlor"), drawing rooms and dining rooms. Dense mahogany, unlike oak and walnut, is more resistant to tunneling beetles and is perfect for detailed carving.

This mahogany oxbow Chippendale desk, circa 1780-1790, has been reproduced many times. The reproductions are known as "Governor Winthrop" desks.

A suite of Chippendale side chairs with square legs from 1770.

Skinner Auctions, Inc.

Mahogany's debut marked a crucial turning point, as pieces were being identified more and more by creator rather than monarch. "That chair is by Mr. So-and-So" became the often-heard word-of-mouth advertisement. One particular cabinetmaker whose name was mentioned more than others would eventually achieve legendary status in the world of antiques. Mr. Thomas Chippendale, the superstar of English furniture, was born in Yorkshire around 1718. As a youth, he went to London to seek his fortune and, in 1753, opened a shop at 60 Saint Martin's Lane. Although the shop no longer exists, an elegant plaque proclaims the master's former location, near the famous St. Martin's-in-the-Field Church.

Mr. Chippendale, besides being a fine artisan, was also a savvy businessman. His artistic manifesto, published three times, fashioned his legendary status. *The Gentleman and Cabinet-Maker's Director* appeared in 1754, 1755 and 1762. Competitors such as Nice and Mayhew printed similar books, but Chippendale's tome became the bible for good taste.

The Gentleman and Cabinet-Maker's Director, resembling modern "how-to" primers, looked like a cookbook filled with recipes for furniture styles. The first edition had over 160 designs, while the third presented over 200 drawings, illustrated design trademarks, and methods for constructing tables, fire screens, beds, chairs and other items.

George Washington was quite a fan of Chippendale and had several Chippendale-style pieces in Mount Vernon.

This is a definitive Chippendale side chair. This walnut carved chair from Philadelphia, circa 1755-1770, displays robust cabriole legs, ball-and-claw feet, and a carved, pierced splat.

Another definitive example of the Chippendale side chair. Note the pad feet on this piece.

The Queen Anne Style
(Renamed "The English Style")

Since Mr. Chippendale appreciated perfection, his book endorsed the Queen Anne style, which he christened the "English style." This tactic proved one of his most successful career moves because the Queen Anne style remained cherished among the British and Colonists.

The Chippendale version of Queen Anne or "English style" had a slightly different flourish. Earlier furnishings from the 1720s and 1730s, as you recall, were more delicate, with thin cabriole legs. The Chippendale versions became even stouter and more highly carved.

A cherry tilt-top table, circa 1760-1780. The support where the top attaches to the base is charming known as a "bird cage."

Chippendale Trademarks

RIBBON/RIBBAND BACK CHAIRS

Chippendale updated the Hogarth chair from Queen Anne days by creating stouter lines and additional flourishes. What formerly had been a solid wooden vase- or fiddle-shaped splat became a carved spiraling ribbon motif. These splats are called ribbon/ribband backs. (I have seen both terms used. Use the one you prefer.) Today a ribbon/ribband back Chippendale chair, with or without arms, terminating with finely detailed ball-and-claw feet, best demonstrates the artisan's genius.

PEMBROKE TABLES WITH MARLBOROUGH LEGS

Even though Chippendale appreciated the long-established Queen Anne style, he realized that innovative designs kept sales flourishing. Clothing manufacturers do the same with perennially changing skirt heights and tie widths. Chippendale cleverly "borrowed" several designs from China because the British, Europeans and Colonists were passionate about anything Chinese. Straight legs borrowed from China were used for chairs and tables and were promptly given the very proper English name Marlborough legs. These legs captured second place in popularity after cabriole models.

The Pembroke table, which incorporated Marlborough legs, remains as popular today as in the 1700s. An enchanting account about its origin has floated for centuries. (Although the tale may not be true, it makes learning fun.) We've all seen movies with scenes highlighting majestic English manor houses whose dining rooms seem as sprawling as Wal-Mart parking lots. With Lord and Milady sitting at opposite ends of an enormous table, hollering must have been a necessity at meals. According to legend, a fashionable duchess who destested breakfasting in such vastness came up with better idea. She asked Chippendale to create a smaller table for repasts in her boudoir.

The petit breakfast table featured straight Marlborough legs and drop leaves that opened for meals. Rumor insists that Mr. Chippendale's novelty was christened "Pembroke table" in honor of its sponsor, the Duchess of Pembroke. Who knows if this is merely an antiques fable? Nevertheless, many Pembroke tables, whether genuine or reproduction, still adorn homes everywhere.

Other Chinese Motifs

Many Chinese designs were illustrated in *The Gentleman and Cabinet-Maker's Director*. Latticework adapted from pagodas bedecked chair backs. Another lovely design was gilded-framed looking glasses (mirrors) festooned with miniature Chinese pagodas complete with latticework and birdhouse. A canopy bed enshrined under a pagoda-shaped canopy really captured Chinese flavor.

Such Chinese patterns had far-reaching influence. The fanfare for Chinese Chippendale led to the production of fine European wallpaper based on colorful oriental themes. Such wallpaper has remained so chic that President Reagan's bedroom in the White House was decorated with a fine example depicting flowers and birds.

The Gothic Style

The Gothic taste proved less popular than other Chippendale works. Rather than lattice or ribbon/ribband chair backs, pointed arches repeating medieval Gothic architecture became this Chippendale motif. Gothic seems to have been too reminiscent of churches, and the pointed backs weren't particulary user friendly. No doubt these shortcomings explained Gothic's weak appeal.

The French Taste

Chippendale proved himself the ultimate hero of a Tale of Two Antiques Cities when it came to this landmark design. Paris and the nearby palace of Versailles were the basis for the "French Taste." This design followed Rococo, which in French comes from "rocaille" for "rock," and "coquille," meaning "shell." By the 1750s, chic Parisians following Madame du Pompadour—the premier pacesetter of the mid-1700s—preferred Rococo, which became known as Louis XV. Cabriole legs similar to those on Queen Anne pieces were the outstanding trademarks of Rococo/Louis XV.

Chippendale adorned chests of drawers and exposed wooden parts of upholstered pieces with shell carving. Knees of cabriole legs and aprons of chairs and tables were also choice locations for embellishments. Chests of drawers curving outwards, known as bow fronts, were comely examples of the French Taste. To add even more sumptuousness, the exposed wooden frames of chairs or sofas were often gilded.

Skinner Auctions, Inc.

Yankee cabinetmakers made few chest-on-chests, but
this 1770 cherry specimen is a spectacular example.

The French Taste style was better received than Gothic, which comes as no surprise, since the British always loved French designs, but these labor-intensive pieces were affordable only for the extremely wealthy. Around a century later, during the reign of George III's granddaughter, Queen Victoria, a machine-made version of Chippendale's French Taste or Rococo finally became the rage in Britain, America and, not surprisingly, for the second time in France.

Mr. Chippendale's book tremendously increased business, and in time made him a legend. His shop crafted furniture for the rich and famous of his century, including the renowned Shakespearian actor David Garrick (1717-1779). Eventually the public called the various

Renowned cabinetmaker John Goddard made this mahogany drop leaf table in Newport, R.I., between 1760 and 1775. Notice the three-dimensional quality of the ball-and-claw feet and the slightly clunky cabriole legs.

Skinner Auctions, Inc.

A superb mahogany Chippendale slant-front desk. This 1770 to 1780 crème de la crème antique features cut-out square bracket feet.

motifs highlighted in the primer "Chippendale." Rarely will you hear the term "Chinese style" used for English gilt looking glasses in the Chinese taste dating from the 1700s. Rather "Chinese Chippendale" has become the accepted terminology, and the same holds true for his other motifs.

Thanks to his book, the cabinetmaker's fame crossed the Atlantic, enlightening American craftsmen about the smartest styles. Chippendale's designs quickly dignified patrician quarters from Boston to Charleston.

A Widely Copied Style

Here's another fascinating point about Mr. Chippendale. If he made even a tenth of the furniture that's said to be his, the Master would still be working in his London shop day and night. Probably only 10 percent of what has been labeled as made in his shop on Saint Martin's Lane actually was. Here's how provenance (the history of an antique) helps authenticate genuine Chippendale pieces. Harewood House in the Yorkshire region of England has written accounts dating from 1772 that reference purchasing furniture from Chippendale.

As competing cabinetmakers followed Chippendale designs, the superstar astutely acknowledged that imitation was high flattery. Benjamin Randolph (1721-1791), a celebrated Philadelphia artisan, made a Chippendale French table that would have pleased the master. The original owner paid about 94 pounds for this 1760 masterpiece. At the time, this sum was equal to 15 percent of the cost of an elegant city house.

At the height of Chippendale's career, archeological digs conducted on Roman ruins were about to revolutionize home décor. Mr. Chippendale, ever a talented businessperson and artist extraordinaire, remained adaptable, so his story continues in the next chapter.

Chapter 9
"Heppleton": A Hepplewhite and Sheraton Medley

Time and again, historical events have launched trends. During the mid-1700s, the discovery of an ancient catastrophe triggered two superb styles that have justifiably become antique icons.

In 79 AD, two Roman cities experienced a mammoth tragedy that killed 2,000 citizens. Pompeii and nearby Herculaneum, located about 14 miles south of modern Naples, Italy, were buried under ash from Mount Vesuvius. This hermetically sealed buildings and furnishings, leaving the site in a remarkable state of preservation.

When the ruins of Pompeii and Herculaneum were unexpectedly discovered in 1748, archeological digs for studying and salvaging Roman artifacts commenced in full force. Pompeii especially proved a windfall because other ancient cities, such as Herculaneum and Imperial Rome, were in a constant state of modernization, which routinely obliterated ancient relics.

The rescued Roman artifacts were tagged "antiques." (By the late 1800s, this term, as you recall, had also evolved into our modern jargon for old things.) These excavations marked the most significant trendsetting event for decorative arts (the academic term for antiques) since Mr. Polo returned to Venice with his hoard of Chinese artifacts.

The Society of Dilettante, organized in England around 1732 to promote art connoisseurship, added even more momentum to the zeal for antiquity. The word "dilettante" originated from this group, meaning a person who dabbles in art not as a "day job," but as a hobby. The "Grand Tour" of Europe became a must for members to personally experience artistic wonders, much the same way modern college students spend a year abroad. This educational jaunt usually included extended stays in Rome, Venice, Flanders, Holland, Paris and, after their discoveries, Pompeii and Herculaneum.

Robert Adam

A Scottish architect, during his Grand Tour, became enamored while visiting the ruins at Pompeii and Herculaneum. After four years in Italy, Robert Adam (1728-1792) published a book about Roman architecture in 1773. *The Works in Architecture*, his tome with drawings of furniture as well as residences resembling Roman palaces, handsomely introduced the neoclassical style to an awaiting public.

The Neoclassical Style

Thanks to Mr. Adam, "neoclassical" remains a mighty significant term for architecture and antiques. The prefix "neo" means new, as in revival or comeback, while "classical" refers to artifacts and architecture from antiquity when Rome, Greece and Egypt were world powers. "Classical" usually conjures up visions of togas, fig leaves and folks running around in the most antique costume of all, their birthday suits. But let's keep this at an artistic level and ponder the architecture of those days. Most likely, temples—with their symmetry and trademark columns—come to mind. Those cylindrical supports held up many a classical roof, from temples to palaces, and are the key to recognizing classical and neoclassical architecture.

Mr. Adam designed some remarkable neoclassical buildings, so let's regard him as the "Frank Lloyd Wright" of the 1700s. His Adelphi Terrace in London was famed for arches reminiscent of the glorious Pantheon temple in Rome. Although he also designed neoclassical furnishings, Mr. Adam is mainly revered as an unparalleled neoclassical architect.

It's easy to confuse Adam's name with two Yankee gentlemen. Keep in mind that Robert Adam had no "s" in his last name. He was an architect and author, not a politician like U.S. presidents John Adams and his son John Quincy Adams. Ironically, however, the two presidents resided in the foremost neoclassical residence of the United States, the White House, whose design was inspired by Robert Adam.

The Adam introduction of the neoclassical style influenced artists, potters, silversmiths and cabinetmakers. Mr. Chippendale, ever the good businessman, followed the architect's example by producing fine neoclassical furniture. Many consider pieces from his mature years his finest. His son, Thomas the younger (1749-1822), continued the family tradition of crafting superb furniture.

Even matchless china maker Josiah Wedgwood was smitten with the style for which Adam was so acclaimed. The potter initiated his highly celebrated and especially neoclassical line Jasperware with one nod to decorum. The china legend fretted that the scantily attired classical figures on his porcelain would be scandalous. As a special consideration for female sensitivities, very non-neoclassical fig leaves became standard Wedgwood embellishments.

Mr. Adam remains a celebrity in the antiques world because he brought neoclassicism to Britain and ultimately to America. In France, the style was called "le Gout Grec" (Greek Taste), while the furniture is known as the Louis XVI style, in honor of King Louis XVI of France. Two of the architect's most loyal apostles wrote design books unveiling two much-admired neoclassical styles.

George Hepplewhite

George Hepplewhite (?-1786) mastered furniture in Lancaster, England, and in Chippendale's footsteps, trekked off to London to establish his own legacy. No furniture made by his own hands has ever been identified, but antiquers are indebted to Mrs. Hepplewhite for promoting her husband's legacy.

In 1788, Hepplewhite's widow, Alice, published *The Cabinet Maker and Upholsterer's Guide.* In the preface, Hepplewhite straightforwardly credits Robert Adam for the neoclassical style. Bravo, Mr. Hepplewhite!

Hepplewhite-style furniture is fragile-looking compared to Chippendale or earlier Queen Anne

A Hepplewhite chest of drawers made of cherry ("poor man's mahogany") and mahogany veneer, circa 1820. Notice the flaring feet, called French feet.

Skinner Auctions, Inc.

Skinner Auctions, Inc.

The Hepplewhite style perfected the sideboard. This masterpiece dates from 1790 to 1800. The square tapered legs and inlay are outstanding.

pieces. Hepplewhite designs, customarily crafted from mahogany, were usually small tables, chairs or writing desks.

Hepplewhite Trademarks

SPADE FEET

Hepplewhite hit another artistic home run when it came to devising legs for furniture. His typical leg was square at the top and gradually narrowed or tapered toward the bottom. Near the base, all four sides jutted out slightly in the shape of a square shovel, forming what became known as spade feet.

SHIELDBACK CHAIRS

Shield-shaped urns, so prominent in classical artifacts, became a dominant Hepplewhite trait. Chair backs repeating outlines of urns scored big with blue bloods hankering for chic neoclassical adornment. Such chairs became another Hepplewhite trademark design, initiating another generic name enduring to this very day: "shieldback chairs."

MARQUETRY

Unlike Chippendale, Hepplewhite eliminated carving on furniture.

The robust Chippendale ball-and-claw feet and Rococo shells never graced fragile Hepplewhite pieces. Instead, various hued woods were inlayed/fitted into background mahogany. Called marquetry, this decoration was a wooden mosaic usually depicting seashells or bell-flowers.

TAMBOUR FRONTS

Hepplewhite had several feathers in his design cap including shieldback chairs and square tapered legs; however, tambour fronts added a peacock plume. Tambours were narrow vertical strips of wood glued onto a heavy background cloth placed near the rear of writing surfaces. These upright wooden curtains on desks elegantly hid the little cubbyholes and short drawers so handy for writing supplies. This innovation was so winning that by the late 1800s a modification of the tambour emerged. The furniture pieces that incorporated these machine-produced horizontal curtains became known as "roll-top desks."

The Hepplewhite style enjoyed a huge following in both Great Britain and the United States from 1790 to about 1820. During Hepplewhite's heyday, another neoclassical style became equally esteemed. In fact, we could say that Hepplewhite and its cousin were truly artistic soul mates.

Thomas Sheraton

The second majestic style inspired from antiquity was based on the work of Thomas Sheraton (1751-1806), a con-

A Hepplewhite mahogany inlaid desk and bookcase, known as a "secretary desk," circa 1790 to 1810.

Skinner Auctions, Inc.

temporary of Hepplewhite and, naturally, a fellow admirer of Robert Adam. Around 1790, London beckoned the Englishman to establish his career there. Sheraton was known to be a highly skilled cabinetmaker, but sadly, none of his furniture has ever been authenticated. His fame rests upon the *Cabinet and*

A mahogany Hepplewhite lady's tambour desk dating from 1794 to 1809. Notice its sliding door (tambour) front and its inlay design, both trademarks of the Hepplewhite style.

A rural Hepplewhite-style cherry sugar chest from the early 1800s. In those days, sugar was expensive, so the sugar chest served as a sugar safe.

Upholsterer's Drawing Book, published in parts from 1791 to 1794. Sheraton's highly respected work is a manual of furniture designs, including construction details. His publication did very well in Britain and in its former North American colony, the newly formed United States.

Sheraton, like Hepplewhite, loved mahogany, but variations between the two styles existed. Sheraton chairs had square-shaped backs, usually with three horizontal bars (splats), instead of oval shield-shaped backs. Sheraton legs, unlike Hepplewhite legs, were really nothing new, but rather a stylish continuation of rounded legs that had been around for centuries. The legs were easy to turn on a lathe and, in a few decades, would easily adapt to mass production.

Since both Hepplewhite and Sheraton styles are neoclassical and primarily used mahogany, the two strongly resemble each other, which makes distinguishing them somewhat challenging.

The trick for remembering legs shapes is opposite of what is stated about backs in the Loomism above. Hepplewhite advocated square-shaped legs, while Sheraton used rounded legs. This can be confusing, but the good news is that in the late 1700s and early 1800s, many cabinetmakers shared our bewilderment. Even though they followed the two masters' books, designs got mixed. Hepplewhite shieldbacked chairs were created with rounded legs, and so on.

Loomism

Sheraton, which features square-shaped chair backs, begins with the letter "s." Hepplewhite, which has urn-shaped or rounded chair backs, contains the letters wh, as in wheel. Thus, Sheraton = square-shaped, and Hepplewhite = wheel (round)-shaped.

A Sheraton-style chest of drawers with cherry legs and maple drawer fronts. This is an early example of the mirror being an attached part of the lower chest of drawers.

Skinner Auctions, Inc.

An 1810 Sheraton mahogany tall-post tester bed.

Skinner Auctions, Inc.

A country walnut and cherry Sheraton chest of drawers from the early 1800s. Notice the turned rounded legs.

Garth's Auctions, Inc.

A Sheraton mahogany sideboard from the early 1800s.

Garth's Auctions, Inc.

A mahogany veneer Sheraton sofa from Massachusetts or New Hampshire.

Skinner Auctions, Inc.

"Heppleton"

Don't worry about making a distinction between Hepplewhite and Sheraton. Just think of it as "Heppleton." You'll still be ahead of 99 percent of the population. Take this affectionate nickname seriously because cabinet makers did indeed mix the two styles, thus creating "Heppleton" pieces.

Federal

In the United States, there is a tendency to label American Hepplewhite or Sheraton furniture as "Federal." In my antiques book, Federal refers to the 1790s, when America's national government was started and is not a furniture style. The term "Federal" does indeed sound swanky, but use Hepplewhite, Sheraton, or "Heppleton" to be more accurate.

In New York City in the early 1800s, a cabinetmaker named Duncan Phyfe (1768-1854) carried out Sheraton and Hepplewhite neoclassical designs to perfection. Duncan Phyfe is famous for card tables with flip tops that doubled the surface area when opened. He used mahogany in the shape of a lyre (another favor-

Loomism

"Heppleton" (a Hepplewhite/Sheraton combination) features a neoclassical style with square-tapered or rounded legs with incised fluted carving (like a Greek or Roman column) and rounded or square backs.

A Sheraton style flame-birch and mahogany veneer card table, circa 1810. The reeded legs are characteristic of Sheraton style.

Skinner Auctions, Inc.

Skinner Auctions, Inc.

**Three incredible card tables, all dating from 1800 to 1825. The center
table is Sheraton, and the other two are Hepplewhite.**

ite neoclassical design) as the base for many tables. Today, American
museums hoard his work, but you can find affordable 1930s copies at
most antique malls or shops.

Hepplewhite, Sheraton, or "Heppleton" continued as late as the
1820s in the United States. In the next chapter, you will discover how
the Empire style, based on "Heppleton" designs, conquered America.

Chapter 10

Empire:
The Return of the Toga

From the early 1800s to 1850, the Empire style, a neoclassical cousin of Hepplewhite and Sheraton, thoroughly conquered America. Empire motifs influenced designs for furniture, houses, buildings and even dresses. And, of course, no self-respecting artist in those days would ever have crafted a statue of our first President in any other manner than Empire. Now you know why sculptures from the early days of the Republic rarely portrayed George Washington in knickers but rather as a Roman emperor complete with toga.

Origin of the Empire Style

The Empire style was born in France during the fading days of the French Revolution. Beginning in 1789, mobs created a bloodbath in France using a recently invented machine that dramatically sped up executions. Thousands were sent to the Place de la Concorde in central Paris for a rendezvous with Madame Guillotine. By 1795, the havoc had ended, but suffering lingered throughout the country. Thousands of innocents had been beheaded, including well-meaning Louis XVI; his unjustly maligned wife, Marie Antoinette; and their young son, Louis XVII. Rebels also devastated the artistic heritage of France. Chateaux and churches throughout the country were heavily damaged or torched. Scars still remain even in the 21st century. The façade of the Cathedral of Saint Jean in Lyon has many stone saints that have been headless since those violent times.

Directoire

In 1795 a modified Republic was installed in Paris, which brought about many changes, including home décor. Directoire, a design named after the infant government, basically continued the previous Louis XVI style. Since the earlier style was named after the deceased monarch, cabinetmakers needed a glittering new label to boost sales. "Directoire" was not only politically correct, but sounded sophisticated to the throngs who yearned for a return to the gentility of the pre-Revolutionary days known as the Ancien Régime.

During the Directoire, a young Corsican general named Napoleon Bonaparte (1769-1821) rose to power in France. In 1799, Bonaparte overthrew the government, creating a military dictatorship. Napoleon, ever nervous about mobs, did not want a rendezvous with Madame Guillotine. Under his power, the monarchy, following a slightly different format, was restored to France. In 1802 Napoleon created the French Empire, rendering him far more exalted than a mere king had ever been.

On December 2, 1804, the Imperial Coronation took place at the Cathedral of Notre Dame in Paris, where the Pope had planned to officiate. However, as Pius VII held the jeweled tiara over Napoleon, the Corsican irreverently grabbed the headpiece and proceeded to crown himself Emperor and his wife Empress. This cheeky maneuver was Napoleon's way of proclaiming his power to the world.

A look into Napoleon's background helps explain the Empire style associated with his rule. The Bonaparte clan from Corsica could hardly have been deemed genuine French, since the island, although French, had formerly been Italian. In addition, the family actually had to learn French and, even more shocking, was lower-end nobility. Such an unpalatial upbringing must have created a feeling of inferiority and prompted Napoleon's great ambitions that ranged from battling wars to furnishing Imperial residences.

As French homes were bedecked with Directoire touches, Hepplewhite and Sheraton still dominated decorating tastes in Britain and America because Directoire was too short-lived to really take off in those countries.

French Empire Trademarks
ALL THINGS EGYPTIAN

As you learned in the last chapter, ancient Greece and Rome were the main sources for neoclassicism. Although Egypt was part of the classical world, Pompeii had intrigued the public more until 1798, when Napoleon conquered the land of the Pharaohs. When Egyptian artifacts arrived in Paris, suddenly anything Egyptian became as fashionable as Pompeiian relics had been in the 1760s. The French Empire style, unlike Napoleon, was about to conquer the world!

In reality, French Empire was a flamboyant continuation of the neoclassical Louis XVI era and the later, short-lived Directoire period. Legs for tables and other pieces were often classically shaped columns. Another important trademark came from stone monuments dating from classical times. The Sphinx, resembling a Pharaoh's head on a body of a lion with claw feet, enthralled everyone. Soon claw feet became an Empire icon bedecking everything from chairs to beds.

MAHOGANY'S RULE

Mahogany, the premier wood for Empire, was perfect for the robust style central to military themes. Tables often resembled drums, while many fashionable rooms were adorned in striped wallpaper reminis-

Skinner Auctions, Inc.

A fine early Empire pier mahogany table made in Boston around 1815 to 1825. It is purely French in design, especially with its ormolu decorations on the top of the columns and the winged griffins on the apron. The three gilded metal candelabrums from the same period were quite popular during Empire's heyday.

cent of tents used for housing soldiers. No doubt the Emperor, ever aware of fickle loyalty towards monarchs, wanted his furnishings to demonstrate his supremacy.

ORMOLU

Ormolu, especially as claw feet, embellished many Empire pieces. This alloy resembling gold was a mixture of brass and other metals and was also known as bronze doré or gilded bronze. Frequently, casters were discreetly hidden in the hollow underside of claw feet to ease moving. Ormolu laurel wreaths mounted on fronts and sides of cabinets and desks were another stylish addition. Besides being ornamental, ormolu protected wooden parts from scratching or denting, as even in Napoleonic times, furniture was still being carted back and forth from country homes to Parisian town houses, known as hotels. An urban residence near the Imperial Court was necessary if an aristocrat intended to remain in Napoleon's benevolence.

The Empress Josephine

The Empress Josephine wins the honor of being the greatest trendsetter in the world of antiques. A gracious hostess, Napoleon's wife was especially kind to relatives of Louis XVI who returned to France during the Empire. Besides her compassionate nature, Josephine had discriminating taste that has withstood the test of time.

Josephine's chateau, Malmaison, located in the suburbs of Paris, exemplifies what the French call "le bon gout," meaning style and taste. This Empire masterpiece open to the public will take your breath away. At Malmaison, Greek, Roman and Egyptian motifs abound everywhere—from the columned entrance of the chateau to her husband's study, which resembles a colorful field tent. Josephine's presence is felt even two centuries later in the dining room bedecked with black and white marble floor, and walls emblazoned with Roman themes. During summer, roses bloom in surrounding gardens, all descendents of her originals.

Even though Napoleon left Josephine for a younger woman, he remained her most ardent admirer. The Emperor emphatically stated that his fall from power began when he divorced the Empress. His union with Josephine produced no heir, so Napoleon married Marie-Louse (the niece of Marie Antoinette!). This alliance yielded a son, Napoleon II, who died young. Reading the chronicle of the Bonapartes reveals how complicated and surprising fate can truly be. Hortense, Josephine's daughter from her first marriage, married Napoleon's brother, Joseph. Their son (Josephine's grandson and Napoleon's nephew) increased Napoleonic fame and fueled his grandmother's legend. The remainder of this fascinating tale unfolds in a later chapter and, of course, involves another antique style.

Georges Jacob

Following is an account about the celebrated French cabinetmaker Georges Jacob (1739-1814), whom I call "the French Chippendale." Jacob crafted various styles of furniture from the superornate Rococo to the angular neoclassical lines of Empire. The adaptable cabinetmaker began crafting fine furniture during the reign of Louis XV. During the Louis XVI and Directoire years, his stature grew even more. But his Empire pieces were considered his masterworks and today are proudly displayed in French museums. How the artisan escaped the guillotine during the Revolution is utterly amazing, since many poor souls with any association whatsoever with the Ancien Regime ended up at the Place de la Concorde.

The British were Napoleon's biggest foe; between 1793 and 1815 Britain and France were constantly battling. Napoleon's fall was swift, with one defeat leading to another. Finally, the British permanently exiled him to the island of St. Helena in the South Atlantic, where he died in 1821. To paraphrase Shakespeare, "The good men do often lies buried with them," but Napoleon, thanks to Josephine, managed to leave some Empire splendor behind as a legacy.

There is little doubt that King George III hated Napoleon as much as he loathed losing his former American colony. Besides keeping his regal sight focused on France, the king and his wife, Queen Charlotte, fretted about their eldest son, the Prince of Wales. The future George IV was quite a philanderer and did much to upset his parents. His London home, Carlton House, showcased the latest from Paris, which truly antagonized his ma and pa, but the London swells ardently followed his taste. Empire furniture and dresses with high waistlines appeared in swanky London drawings rooms and, in no time whatever, the Empire style reached the United States.

Regency

What vexed the British was how this new style could possibly be called Empire, a name glorifying the archenemy. Designations such as "Greek" or "antique" style were coined to avoid any association with Napoleon. In time, the dilemma ended quite stylishly, since English furniture from the early 1800s became known as "Regency." This term referred to the years 1811 to 1820, when the future George IV acted as regent, or substitute ruler, for his insane father. Think of Regency as the English version of Empire with touches of Hepplewhite and Sheraton. Thus, chairs still featured shield backs and square tapered legs, all courtesy of Mr. Hepplewhite.

Loomism

Think of Regency as the English version of Empire with touches of Hepplewhite and Sheraton.

In 1807, a famous novelist, Thomas Hope, following Mr. Chippendale's success, published *Household Furniture and Interior Design*, which showcased the furniture of his fabulous mansion. His pieces were basically British interpretations of French Empire, using straight lines, claw feet, ormolu ornamentation, and dark, glossy woods like mahogany. Since his death, his fame seems to have diminished, which brings up an intriguing point.

As you read this section, keep in mind that few, if any, cabinetmakers achieved the prominence of Chippendale, Hepplewhite or Sheraton. Thus, no new styles were named after craftsmen. Although several cabinetmakers such as Thomas Shearer enjoyed success, time has somehow erased their former prominence. When it comes to immortality, logic sometimes doesn't apply. Thus, English Empire-style pieces from the late days of George III or the reign of George IV are still called Regency. That elegant sounding name helped maintain the appeal of furnishings from this era.

As Regency conquered England, Hepplewhite and Sheraton in the United States were still highly favored, despite their English heritage. The early days of the United States—roughly from the Treaty of Paris ending the American Revolution until 1825—have been called the Federal Era. Sometimes American Hepplewhite and American Sheraton pieces are inaccurately branded "Federal." The term is appropriate for history but not furniture. As I pointed out previously, to be more precise and professional, use the terms Hepplewhite, Sheraton or, if you wish, "Heppleton."

President George Washington's farewell address advised citizens to remain neutral in world politics by avoiding "entangling alliances." The young nation felt great hostility towards its former mother country but much admiration for France. Yankees never forgot that France had been an ally during the American Revolution. Louis XVI helped fund the war effort not out love for democracy, but rather to attack rival George III. America's third president, Thomas Jefferson, became a great Francophile, or a big fan of France. Jefferson had been minister in Paris just before the French Revolution and brought back shiploads of French articles, including wine and furnishings, which greatly enhanced the American passion for French fashions.

Continued hostility between Britain and the United States resulted in the War of 1812, which could easily be called "The American Revolution, Part II." On August 24, 1814, British troops arriving in Washington D.C. burned the Executive Mansion and other government buildings. One grand treasure in the president's house escaped destruction. Legendary First Lady Mrs. James Madison, before leaving the doomed mansion, ordered the portrait of George Washington cut from its frame. Minutes before the invading troops arrived, "Queen Dolley" escaped with the painting. In a few years, the charred stone walls of the rebuilt Executive Mansion were painted white, giving birth to the nickname the "White House." And today, thanks to Dolley, Gilbert Stuart's famous portrait of the general hangs in the East Room of the White House.

American Empire

You can understand how British culture and artifacts at that time were not nearly as welcomed as arrivals from France. Savvy American merchants shied away from applying the names of British styles to imported furnishings. Some clever retailer came up with the idea of keeping the original French name, and Empire became the rage from Maine to Georgia and eventually to the tip of Florida. The triumphs of the Louisiana Purchase of 1803 and the War of 1812 reinforced the belief that America was an empire expanding westward from the Atlantic Coast across North America.

Empire designs neoclassicalized America from 1810 to as late as 1850. (Remember that dates concerning styles are never exact.) Everything from bank buildings with Greek columns to card tables with claw feet fell under the influence of the Empire style.

Three beautiful early Empire mahogany pieces: a chest of drawers, a breakfast table and a candlestick stand. The table's legs have acanthus leaf carvings. The portrait "Lady Holding a Pink Rose" is of the Empire period.

American Empire varied slightly from French Empire. Such differences seem perfectly logical, since America's heritage was more British than French. American Empire had more carving than ormolu decoration. For example, claw feet on French pieces were mostly ormolu, while American models were usually carved wood.

The midsections of table bases were frequently carved to resemble pineapples, while cornucopias, also known as horns of plenty, were carved into the wooden scroll arms of sofas. Acanthus leaf carvings, which originated in antiquity, were another esteemed motif that graced legs of tables and chairs. American Empire, like French Empire, used classical columns for table legs and other pieces.

American Empire, like their French counterparts, favored mahogany. On many chests of drawers, sides were crafted from mahogany, while choice crotch mahogany veneer covered drawer fronts usually made from less expensive pine. This technique made the whole case appear totally crafted from upscale timber. The beautifully grained strips of wood came from mahogany trees where a limb joined the trunk. The veneer was cut at an angle to create a feather design.

Cottage furnishings (an 1800s expression for "low-end"), sides of chests of drawers were made from less expensive and locally grown cherry, which resembled mahogany-veneered drawer fronts. As pointed out earlier, in the early 1800s, cherry was

A fine grain and crotch mahogany sideboard, circa 1820. Notice the carved claw feet.

The two silk needlepoint pictures date from the early Empire period.

often called "the poor man's mahogany" because this timber was less expensive but shared the same rosé hue.

American Empire can be rather complex due to this style's three distinct phases. Let's look at sofas representing the three periods: early, middle and late.

EARLY EMPIRE

An early Empire sofa made between 1810 and 1830 was totally hand-made and rather ornate compared to later models. Examples from this period have finely carved hairy animal claw feet and cornucopia carvings on both wooden arm rests. Upholstery was usually velvet or horsehair, a very durable covering first used in the late 1700s.

MID-EMPIRE

A mid-Empire sofa dates from 1830 to as late as 1840. Its carvings were far less precise, making the claw feet and arms less detailed. Examples from the 1830s were transitional because some parts, such as wooden interiors, were machine made. By the mid-1830s, the attitude "the faster the better," had become a maxim of the Industrial Revolution. The laborer on the assembly line was swifter, and perhaps less conscientious, than the individual cabinetmaker who crafted early Empire pieces.

LATE EMPIRE

The third period of American Empire marks a major turning point in American furniture. This furniture was mostly machine made. A

Skinner Auctions, Inc.

A mid-Empire vignette typical of the 1820s and 1830s. The table in the foreground is for sewing. Its curved fabric sack was handy for holding fabric. The daybed was known as a "Recamier" after Madame Recamier, who made them chic in Napoleonic France. The lyre-base table beneath the mirror is a card table whose top, when opened, doubles in size. The tea set, with its urn-shaped bodies, is of the Empire period. The gilt mirror was placed over the mantel and has often been called a "Dolley Madison" mirror after the beloved First Lady.

mass-produced late Empire sofa has far less detail compared to earlier versions. This phase brought about a name for late Empire pieces that was not very complimentary.

Pillar and Scroll

Mass-produced late Empire furnishings earned the rather disdainful title "Pillar and Scroll." By 1840, the Industrial Revolution had changed the way household goods were made. Glass, clocks, silver plate and furniture were mostly machine produced. But machines couldn't duplicate the complex curves and lines in claw feet and neoclassical columns; they were only able to copy their general shape or outline. Consequently, manufacturers could only produce large pillars for the columns, while claw feet emerged as scroll feet. Thus, the late Empire style was the given the uncomplimentary name "Pillar and Scroll."

Late Empire, the first style to be mass produced, catered to the rising power of middle-class Americans. Social as well as technological changes were taking place everywhere in the young nation. Since the signing of the Treaty of Paris, the patrician set, including Jefferson, Washington, Madison and Monroe had ruled the infant Republic. But the election of Andrew Jackson to the presidency in 1828 revealed

Skinner Auctions, Inc.

that America was becoming a modern culture. "Old Hickory" was not an Eastern blue blood but a Westerner from the Tennessee frontier. Jackson's presidency has been called "The First Age of the Common Man," a graceful way of referring to the ascent of the middle class. Thus, late Empire, the first furniture to be totally machine made and far more affordable than handmade versions, became a status symbol for middle-class parlors all across America.

A mid-Empire sofa and parlor table crafted in mahogany, dating to 1840. The marble top parlor table is also mid-Empire. Such pieces have less detailing than early Empire examples.

In the next chapter, you'll read how the middle class influenced home décor.

Skinner Auctions, Inc.

Late Empire sofas, like this one, circa 1840 to 1850, were often used in entranceways of grand homes.

Chapter 11
The Victorian Era: The Gilded Age

A glimpse into the sweeping political and technological events of the 1800s helps gives a great deal of insight about our not-too-distant ancestors.

Historians, as you recall, have designated the period from 1714 to 1830 in Great Britain as the "Georgian Age," after the four King Georges who ruled that country. During those years, the Queen Anne, Chippendale, Hepplewhite and Sheraton styles were at their pinnacles. The death of George IV in 1830 ended the Georgian Era. When his brother William IV, who succeeded him, died in 1837 without legitimate heirs, their niece became queen, and a whole new epoch began.

The years of the British queen's reign, 1837 to 1901, have been christened the Victorian Age. During that time, the Industrial Revolution created astonishing gains in Britain, France and America. The well-to-do became even more well off, but the phenomenon also elevated masses from the ranks of the poor to the middle class. Tragically, though, there were choppy times. During the 1860s, the United States endured the catastrophic Civil War, and in 1870, the Franco-Prussian War ravaged Paris, as France needlessly and unsuccessfully challenged Germany's growing power.

The Technological Era Begins

The Victorian Era marked the birth of the "Technological Age," which as we are so aware, is still going full force. Numerous inventions such as telegraphs, trains, steamboats, typewriters and other marvels were introduced during this period. Even Queen Victoria got into the fervor for sci-

Early Auction Company

This banquet kerosene lamp made by Mount Washington is from the late 1800s.

entific advancement. On January 14, 1878, Alexander Graham Bell demonstrated his wonder to Her Majesty. She promptly ordered telephones for Osborne House, located on the Isle of Wright in the English Channel.

Another marvel from this era was photography, which vividly demonstrated how technology enhanced the lives of so many. Before Louis Daguerre, only painters could adequately capture a person's likeness. In 1838 when this trailblazer perfected the new-fangled sensation, daguerreotypes became affordable for the masses, a wondrous feat that portraiture never accomplished.

One gentleman achieved much success by becoming the "Richard Avedon" of the mid-1800s. James Presley Ball (1825-1904) was the Victorian equivalent of that highly touted 20th century photographer of the rich and famous. The African-American had one of the best galleries in the United States, located in Cincinnati. Mr. Ball's clientele could easily have been listed in the Who's Who of the mid-1800s. He photographed the family of President Ulysses Grant, opera singer Jenny Lind, and during his 1856 visit to England, added Queen Victoria and author Charles Dickens to his list of famous patrons.

Early Auction Company

This centerpiece with a Webb glass bowl truly sums up the lavishness of the Victorian era.

The Industrial Revolution

Although it's true that modernization devastated the environment, benefits did abound. We antiquers owe this event much gratitude, as you are about to discover. One stunning benefit was a magnificent Art

Movement (which will be discussed shortly) that developed as a revolt against industrialization. Of course, there were other gains, too.

Technology tremendously increased output, which lowered prices for practically everything that previously had been handmade. In preceding centuries, only the wealthy could afford handcrafted items. With the arrival of mass production, for the first time in history more possessions became attainable for much of the populace. In the 1700s, only a person born with a silver spoon in his/her mouth could afford a fine chair or a porcelain tea set. By the mid-1800s, the middle class in both Europe and America had not only the means to splurge but were also eager to flaunt their prosperity. Therefore, possessions became avenues for demonstrating financial achievements and greatly influenced several styles that we are about to encounter.

How Victorians adored large ornate urns! This 40-inch high example is a remarkable work of art made in France around 1900.

Jackson's International Auctions

The "Shop Till You Drop" Era Begins

Victorian days also brought about a beloved pastime that continues to the present. The phrase "shop till you drop" may just have been coined back in the mid-1800s. Consumers of earlier times never experienced the "one-stop" shopping that is the norm today. However, by the mid-1800s, the ever-increasing prosperity of the masses, combined with the avalanche of more reasonably priced machine-made wares revolutionized retailing. Before the Industrial Revolution, merchants specialized in goods because ponderous handcraftsmanship limited available supplies. Con-

The Chinese catered to the Victorian zeal for mother-of-pearl inlay by adding this embellishment to furnishings exported to Europe and the U.S.

Jackson's International Auctionsy

Jackson's International Auctions

This papier-mâché table from the mid-1800s is laden with mother-of-pearl in true Victorian spirit.

sumers went to one shop for gloves, another for china, and so on. Modern retailing was born when posh stores began selling a range of merchandise. Many consider the Bon Marché, founded in Paris in 1865, to be the first department store. However, Chicagoans (including me) would argue that Potter Palmer's (now Marshall Field's) magnificent store on State Street has the honor, since it dates from the 1850s. On the other hand, Philadelphians would proclaim John Wanamaker the retail trailblazer, while Manhattanites would declare A. T. Stewart's marble palace the pioneer. But no matter which bazaar wins the distinction, remember that the Industrial Revolution gave birth to one-stop shopping.

The Ever-Evolving Definition of Antique

In the 1950s and 1960s, most purists still observed the pre-1820 rule pertaining to genuine antiques and sadly dismissed most Victorian articles as riff-raff. But today, even the most rigid experts agree that Victorian pieces are museum caliber. Just check out displays the next time you go museum hopping. Both the Cincinnati Wing at the Cincinnati Art Museum and the Museum of Decorative Arts in Paris proudly showcase antiques from this period, as so many other museums do, too. However, the down side to such ritzy status is the hefty price tags, which limits our choices.

Even napkin rings display the Victorians' love for ornateness. This silver plate napkin ring portrays a child and dog.

Jackson's International Auctions

By now you probably find the subjectivity of what is antique (and isn't) a hoot! Remember Gram saying, "Why do you want that? I threw one out just like it forty years ago?" When I see 20-something collectors selecting 1980s "Retro" rotary telephones, her words al-

Jackson's International Auctions

ways remind me that "antique is in the eye of the beholder." But I'm grateful for the philosophy that one person's trash is another's antique. If we all collected the same stuff, supplies would diminish and prices would go through the roof.

Before looking at the important styles of the Victorian era, one misleading notion pertaining to this era needs to be corrected. Just as the 1700s witnessed several major designs, the same is true with the 1800s. When discussing antiques from

What a lavish décor these Victorian era candelabrums must have seen!

✻

Loomism

Refrain from using the term "Victorian" to describe antiques from Victoria's era, as several distinct styles existed during her reign.

Jackson's International Auctions

Gilded bronze mirrors were the height of fashion during Victorian days.

Victoria's reign, refrain from saying "Victorian." That's like saying American rifles made during the 1860s are "Lincolns." It's more accurate to call them Springfields or Winchesters, etc.

Gilding

By understanding the Victorian philosophy of home decor, you will more easily master the era's main styles. One of the key decorating motifs of this period involved gold. This magical ingredient has jazzed many drab artifacts since its first use in ancient times, but the Victorian era was truly its "golden" age.

Gold has bedecked every type of antique whether furniture, china, books, religious articles or paintings. Long before the birth of Christ, it was known that gold could be beaten into very thin sheets called leaves. Gilding involves applying the leaves to surfaces using a glue-like substance called mordant.

Gilding has always been costly and generally reserved for very special uses. Entire Egyptian mummies were encased in gold leaf. During the Middle Ages, hand-copied books were often illustrated with miniature paintings beautified by gold. In one masterpiece created about 1415, *Les Tres Riches Heures du Duc de Berry*, artists were especially generous with gilt, surrounding the benefactor, the Duke of Berry, with a halo-like background.

By the 1400s and 1500s, architectural elements such as pointed tips on iron fences were given the gilded touch. By the 1600s, artistic history was made when, for the first time, frames encasing paintings were gilded. Before the advent of electricity, this attractive addition to artwork with its mirror-like quality intensified precious artificial lighting, making pictures more visible at night.

A gilded brass gasolier from the days when gas stylishly lit elegant homes.

In the 1700s, the French aristocracy preferred gilded Louis XV and Louis XVI style furniture for their regal residences. As you recall, the peerless 1700s English cabinetmaker Thomas Chippendale designed gilded Chinese-style mirrors. Their gold-leafed frames, like those of paintings, stylishly intensified candlelight, again demonstrating our ancestors' ingenuity.

Gilding finally reached the peak of chicness in the Victorian era. The newly prosperous who wished to parade their privileged cir-

How Victorians loved gilded mirrors! Gilded looking glasses in the 1800s came in an array of styles.

Garth's Auctions, Inc.

Before electricity, wall sconces with mirrors intensified the light produced by candles.

Jackson's International Auctions

This bronze table perfectly exemplifies flamboyant Victorian tastes.

Skinner Auctions, Inc.

cumstances in their homes chose furnishings with flamboyant gilded touches.

Unlike previous generations, Victorians weren't understated in their décor. Some variation of gilding decorated most china, whether crafted by a French Limoges firm such as Haviland or by the celebrated English maker Minton. Gilt also routinely highlighted woodwork and ceilings of grand houses. For Victorians, furniture was not considered top drawer unless some gilding was included. One model of a curio cabinet that Victorians particularly adored duplicated the 1750s Louis XV style right down to its glowing sheath. Another golden touch in dining rooms was gold-plated silver flatware called vermeil, which complemented many a swanky dinner.

In 1873, Mark Twain (1835-1910) wrote *The Gilded Age,* a blockbuster novel whose title chronicled the greed and, indirectly, the decorating tastes of this era. Although officially fiction, innuendo suggests that the plot was based on real-life experiences. From an antiques point of view, Mark Twain coined the name that still defines Victorian decorating, as you are about to discover.

Chapter 12

Victorian, Part I: Rococo Revival

Rococo Revival in France

During the 1840s and the 1850s, Rococo Revival became the first significant trend of the Victorian era. A quick review of French history will give us a keen insight into this ever-popular style.

During the French Revolution, child king Louis XVII succeeded his martyred father, Louis XVI, but tragically died before the atrocity halted. As you recall from the Empire chapter, in the 1790s France had several ineffective governments until Napoleon became Emperor in 1804. After failing to conquer all of Europe, Bonaparte abdicated in 1814. Once again, France became a genuine monarchy. The elder brother of the Louis XVI (and uncle of the boy king) then became the ruling sovereign. The reigns of Louis XVIII and his brother, Charles X, are called the Restoration.

Not surprisingly, a new design for furniture evolved during the Restoration, which was named in the honor of the monarchs. The Louis XVIII/Charles X style essentially followed the Napoleonic/Empire motifs of the early 1800s, but with one difference. Lighter-colored pale cherry or pear woods were popular instead of the Imperial mahogany so prevalent in Empire pieces.

Louis Philippe, the successor of Charles X, lost his throne in 1848. After another gory revolution, a dramatic historical irony emerged. This astonishing tale begins in 1810 when Napoleon I divorced the charming Josephine because their marriage produced no heir. Nevertheless, the Empress triumphed in the game of musical thrones.

When Louis Philippe abdicated, another Napoleon, Napolean III (who was briefly introduced in the Empire chapter) was ascending to power. His blue-blooded background had a twist that not even the first Napoleon could ever have anticipated, as he was the grandson

A French Rococo Revival mantel clock that would have made the Empress Eugénie proud! The glass dome protected the decoration and mechanism.

Forsythes' Auctions

of Josephine from her first marriage to the Vicompte de Beauharnais. Thus, Josephine, in due course, was entitled to the last Imperial laugh. The reign of Napolean III and his beguiling wife, Empress Eugénie, which coincided with Victoria's, was designated the Second Empire, in honor of the First Empire.

In the 1840s, as Josephine's grandson conquered politics, the French searched the past for design inspiration. The sumptuous Louis XVI style of the 1770s and 1780s remained emotionally off-limits because it still all too vividly recalled bread lines and beheadings. The earlier Louis XV/Rococo style was revived because it offered elegant grace without the agonizing reminiscences of the Reign of Terror. And by the mid-1800s, enough time had elapsed to erase the tarnished memories of the authoritarian Louis XV. The Louis XV/Rococo style evoked glorious recollections of a period when France ruled as a world power and shimmering gold and white soirées took place at Versailles.

Victoria, Napoleon III and Eugénie Heal Old Wounds

The Rococo/Louis XV revival entails a major chapter in our Tale of Two Antiques Cities. During the Second Empire, Paris once again dominated the aesthetic universe, where people flocked to study art, food, architecture, fashions and home décor. Another incredible phenomenon occurred. Thanks to Victoria, Napoleon III, and Eugénie, France and Great Britain became allies. The new camaraderie was largely attributable to Victoria, who, as a token of goodwill, returned to France the wagon that originally carried the coffin of Napoleon I. This was a significant diplomatic move because only a few decades earlier the dictator had been determined to conquer England. Today, this cart is displayed at Josephine's Chateau de Malmaison, the incredible Empire masterpiece near Paris that is highlighted in the Empire chapter.

The three greatest trendsetters/diplomats of the 1800s greatly boosted the status of Rococo Revival. Besides being the last word for fashion devotees, this style brought about the unique perk of being politically correct. The unprecedented camaraderie between two former rivals encouraged Londoners all the more to follow Parisian trends.

Rococo Revival in the United States

Shortly before the Civil War devastated the United States, a new chapter was added to our Tale of Two Antiques Cities. When Mrs. Lincoln compared herself to the regal Europeans, she felt inadequate. The First Lady thought perhaps redecorating the White House would be the key to gaining social equality with Queen Victoria and the Empress Eugénie. Upon moving to Pennsylvania Avenue, Mary Todd Lincoln set about to "modernize" the very neoclassical White House. So out went the "Heppleton" and Empire-style furnishings that we discussed in earlier chapters. How Mrs. Lincoln "Rococoized" the Executive Mansion presents a very insightful primer about Rococo Revival. To fully understand the transformation of the Presidential residence, let's take a closer look at Rococo Revival.

A Rococo Revival walnut bed similar to the Lincoln bed in the White House.

Forsythes' Auctions

Rococo Revival Trademarks

DESIGN

Rococo Revival is a later version of Chippendale's "French Style," which was what Rococo Revival was called in Britain and the United States during Victorian times. The term Rococo Revival, which was adopted years later, is more precise, while many designs could fall under the general "French Style" heading.

CLUTTER EVERYWHERE

Rococo Revival lacked the understatement prevalent in 1700s styles. In the mid-1800s, clutter flourished in homes, and nowhere was it more rampant than at 1600 Pennsylvania Avenue or at Buckingham Palace. The prevailing Victorian philosophy toward decorating was to cram as much bric-a-brac, pictures and vases as possible on tables, walls and mantels because "too much is not enough." Mrs. Lincoln followed the "20 Pictures per Table Rule," which suggested refraining from one framed photo on a table when 20 could be packed there. (Although the name of the rule is a product of my imagination, the practice was eagerly followed, nonetheless.)

The early 1800s neoclassical décor of the White House seemed quite old fashioned to most stylish Victorians, including its newest resident, Mrs. L., who promptly "Rococoized" the mansion. A hodge-podge of potted plants, curlicue furniture, competing designs on carpets, upholstery, and draperies, and much gilt decoration on everything from vases to ceilings exploded at 1600 Pennsylvania Ave. After Mrs. Lincoln updated the Executive Mansion, the same decorating upheaval altered many American homes.

THE RETURN OF UNCOMFORTABLE FURNITURE

Through years of collecting, teaching and appraising antiques, I have devised a way to make understanding antique styles a snap. I call it the Sensual Approach to Learning because our senses—whether fingertips, eyes, nose or posterior—can teach many practical facts pertaining to antiques. For example, our cushy area is the best teacher about Rococo Revival. When you're perched on a Rococo Revival chair, your posterior senses that comfort is a not a strong selling point for furniture of this period. (My book *Secrets to Affordable Antiques* reveals more about the Sensual Approach to Learning.)

Do you recall that most seating paraphernalia before the Queen Anne style was rather disagreeable? Well, our posteriors, as I just pointed out, testify how antiques history repeated itself. Rococo Revival marked the comeback of posterior-unfriendly furniture. When I was a young collector, Gram branded antiques as "uncomfortable" whenever I brought up collecting. Surely she recalled Rococo Revival pieces from her childhood. Her very accurate memory recalled dainty chairs with tiny seats and squatty legs. That's why my Flapper grandmother was never fond of antiques.

Here is a fine Rococo Revival sofa made right around the time of the Civil War.

Jackson's International Auctions

ROSES AND ROSEWOOD

Rococo Revival chairs, sofas and tables usually displayed rosewood and roses, the two "R's" that define this style. Rosewood in the mid-1800s became as stylish as mahogany had been in the 1700s, while walnut held second place. Rosewood imported from tropical countries had a pronounced black graining which, much to the delight of Victorians, flamboyantly crisscrossed its mahogany-colored background.

The rose, the second "R" of Rococo Revival, was one of the most popular motifs for furniture, wallpaper, carpets and china, and was often used

This chest of drawers is a fine example of Rococo Revival. Victorians loved marble-topped furniture.

with gilding. Carved roses often decorated the top horizontal wooden crest of chairs or sofas.

MARBLE

Fashionable parlors needed matching sofa(s) and chairs surrounding a central marble-top table. White marble was favored because of its lively contrast to shadowy rosewood and walnut. Since the top usually was buried under myriad vases, pictures and other bric-a-brac, neutral white worked best.

Rococo Revival enjoyed other motifs besides roses. Many competing designs such as leaves, grapes, scrolls and shells were routinely emblazoned on a single piece. Another standard for any stylish dining room or foyer was graceful rounded-back side chairs with carved roses or grapes and leaves. These Victorian icons with the famous cabriole legs and the charming pet names "balloon backs" and "rose backs" are indispensable for Rococo Revival stalwarts and still adorn many homes.

Garth's Auctions, Inc.

John Henry Belter: A Rococo Revival Superstar

Before the comeback of Rococo Revival in the late 20th century, little information was available about a gentleman who combined art with the technology of the Industrial Revolution. During his heyday in the 1850s, John Henry Belter (1804-1863) of New York City reigned as the premier cabinetmaker for the smart set.

Mr. Belter used a laminating process in which several thin strips of rosewood or walnut

This sewing or work table is credited to Mr. Rococo Revival himself: John Henry Belter.

were glued together with the grains running in opposite directions. The plywood-like panels were softened by steaming and then formed into curly shapes. Then decorations such as roses were carved into the glued sheets. Thanks to the renewed fervor for Rococo Revival, Mr. Belter's first-class status is assured, and you can see his masterpieces in many museums.

Vive la France!

The mid-1800s were truly "the Gilded Age." Gold decorated almost everything from teacups to faucets. But Victorians not only liked to gild their possessions but also their vocabulary. They thought that using sophisticated-sounding French terms for everyday household items reflected a refined lifestyle. For example, a debonair Victorian always referred to a "whatnot shelf" as an étagère. The French terminology that the British and Americans so craved left no doubt that Paris was the artistic hub of the cosmos.

Definitive Rococo Revival Pieces

TÊTE À TÊTE

One particular type of Victorian furniture christened with a French

A stylish Rococo Revival walnut bedroom suite including chest of drawers, bed and washstand.

Forsythes' Auctions

name remains the ultimate Victorian frou-frou. In French, tête à tête literally means "head to head," and its French name is very appropriate. An "S" shaped settee resembles two armchairs facing opposite directions but sharing a central armrest. The cultured name discreetly hid its true purpose. This contrivance so conducive for l'amour encouraged spooning, which was Victorian slang that needs no explanation. These delightful accoutrements for the art of courting reveal that our ancestors were less straitlaced than we have been led to believe!

Suites/Suits

Here's one final French expression to relish because you undoubtedly already know it. The term "suite" was adapted from the French and refers to matched sets of dining, parlor or bedroom pieces and other artifacts.

How household furniture progressed from being crafted as single units into matching pieces unveils a beguiling detail about Rococo Revival. Although chairs were crafted in sets long before Columbus first sailed for the New World, most other furniture rarely was. Around 1840, as Rococo Revival was becoming chic, the French started creating matching furniture for parlors, dining rooms and bedrooms.

This Parisian trend continued to transform home decors when it reached England and then the United States. Suddenly everything from sanitary ware (slop jars, pitchers and bowls) to furniture was being manufactured "en suite." Dining suites included a table with myriad chairs, a server, sideboard and china closet. Parlors in fashionable homes had suites with one or more sofas, a gentleman's armchair, a slightly smaller version for milady, and two or more side chairs. Bedroom suites

Forsythes' Auctions

This Rococo Revival armoire/wardrobe was collapsible, which made moving far less agonizing.

came with bed, vanity, bench, washstand, tall chest of drawers, dresser with mirror and anything thing else that could be crammed into the space.

The carriage trade (an 1800s expression for the fashionable set) in Britain and America naturally preferred the French word "suite" to the more humble English term "set." You may have even heard the word suit, which evolved from suite and has the same meaning. The more correct French word for "suite" is "ensemble." The *Larousse French-English Dictionary* states that "suite" in French means "a continuation or one after another." It's interesting to see how badly twisted words become going from one language to another, which is just another argument for using antiques terms in our native tongues.

Before we leave Rococo Revival, one final point about the wondrous effects from the Industrial Revolution needs to be applauded. As I pointed out earlier, this transformation made goods in the 1800s less costly for more and more people. That same marvel perseveres in the 21st century. If most antiques from the Victorian era, the first epoch to benefit from industrialization, had been handmade rather than machine produced, they would be out of reach for most present-day collectors. Thankfully, Victorian-era antiques, including Rococo Revival and our next style, Eastlake, still have friendly price tags when compared to earlier handcrafted mementos.

Chapter 13

Victorian, Part II: Eastlake

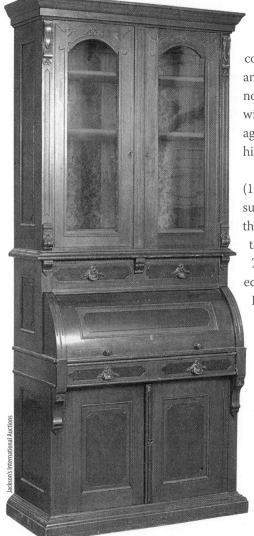

Jackson's International Auctions

The last chapter may have led you to believe that the flamboyant Rococo Revival style enraptured one and all, but by the 1860s a number of nonconformists wanted to do away with such lavishness. An artistic revolt against curlicue furnishings created a highly esteemed antique style.

In the 1860s, Charles Lock Eastlake (1836-1906) became one of the most successful anticurlicue crusaders of the Victorian era. The English architect published *Hints on Household Tastes in Britain* in 1868 and a later edition in the United States in 1872. His bestseller exemplified designs that were quite plain compared to Rococo Revival and even Empire. His artistic beliefs, which took America and Britain by storm in the 1870s and 1880s was christened the Eastlake style.

This secretary bookcase in the Eastlake style was very upscale in the 1880s.

Eastlake-Style Trademarks

STRAIGHT LINES

Just as the Queen Anne style in the previous century had swept away ornate carving, Eastlake did the same in the late 1800s. Fussy decorations including carved roses, grapes and cherubs so prominent on Rococo Revival would never embellish Eastlake pieces. Straight lines define the Eastlake style: chest of drawers, sideboards or other pieces typically had rectangular or boxy shapes.

THE RETURN OF OAK AND WALNUT

Oak and walnut became as favored as they had been in the 1600s. These less expensive timbers made Eastlake more affordable than Rococo Revival pieces crafted from imported rosewood or mahogany.

BURL WALNUT

Since Eastlake believed that the wood itself should be the focal point of any piece, he disdained elaborately carved motifs. Instead, stunning panels of concentrically grained burl walnut embellished his furniture. This choice veneer, which grows in the knots of walnut trees, became the main decoration for drawer fronts. Without this much-needed pizzazz, rectangular Eastlake pieces could easily have resembled orange crates.

Forsythes Auctions

An unusual Eastlake piece in cherry dating from the 1880s.

INCISED CARVING

While Eastlake scorned Rococo Revival carved roses and grapes, some ornamentation besides burl walnut panels met approval. Incised, or low relief carving, became Eastlake's unique trademark. Low relief carving, creating shallow depressions similar to those that spoons leave in ice cream tubs, bestowed Eastlake pieces with low-key panache.

The Eastlake style and the Industrial Revolution developed into a winning duo. By the 1870s, machinery could swiftly and reasonably replicate concave decoration and rectangular shapes. Most Eastlake pieces could also be purchased at "bargain prices" through mail order catalogues (another product of the Industrial Revolution). From Atlantic to Pacific and everywhere in between, Sears Roebuck and Montgomery Ward offered Eastlake stylishness fitting shoestring budgets.

Matching furniture suites, that Rococo Revival novelty, remained chic in the 1870s and 1880s. As a rule, Eastlake parlor suites included a settee (resembling an armchair wide enough for two), one or more armchairs and at least two side chairs. Sets were typically grouped around an Eastlake table that customarily was centrally placed in rooms.

Eastlake bedroom suites usually contained a full-size bed, one or two chests of drawers and a washstand that held that so necessary

Even pump organs received the Eastlake treatment. This 1880s Kimball model has Eastlake trademarks such as walnut and incised carving.

Eastlake parlor suites often had a platform rocker such as the 1880s example on the right.

Here's a smaller Eastlake parlor suite. The settee is not as wide as most.

Jackson's International Auctions

This is a three-piece oak Eastlake bedroom suite that was very popular in the 1880s.

chamber pot. Chests of drawers came in two variations. The first was a low model with two or three drawers and a marble top with or without an attached horizontal mirror. A taller version featured three drawers with a central mirror resting on a small area of marble flanked on either side by little "handkerchief drawers." This example was charmingly branded a "wishbone dresser" since the mirror's side supports resembled that famous part of the Thanksgiving turkey.

A Different Hue for Marble

In Eastlake days, red marble was first choice, since deep hues were considered more flattering to oak and brownish walnut. Small parlor tables complete with red marble became household essentials. In modern homes, pairs of these parlor tables make perfect end tables.

Eastlake Woodwork

Eastlake became so mainstream that American homes built between 1870 and as late as 1910 often had Eastlake trimmings. Lumberyards sold woodwork with ready-made incised carving that would have won Mr. Eastlake's endorsement. Even over a century later, such Eastlake flourishes flanking doors and windows testify to the immense popularity of this style. My nickname for such trim is "eggs and bacon" molding because corners have a circular fried-egg shape, while the incised lines on the vertical and horizontal strips resemble bacon.

Another stunning embellishment in homes is an oak or walnut mantel that copies an Eastlake sideboard or chest of drawers.

The 1870s, 1880s and 1890s were peak decades for Eastlake; but keep in mind that stylish, eclectic Victorians liked mixing styles. For example, Rococo Revival chairs and Eastlake tables graced many parlors along with highly carved and massive cabinets captured in Renaissance Revival, the style described in the next chapter.

This beautiful 1885 sideboard, which mixes Eastlake and Renaissance Revival motifs, was originally for a posh dining room.

Jackson's International Auctions

Chapter 14

Victorian, Part III: Renaissance Revival

Manufacturers have always tried to entice the affluent with the most up-to-date selections for their homes. Similar marketing strategies continue every year when carmakers annually unveil new models. Even though Rococo Revival and Eastlake were very much in vogue during the Victorian era, manufacturers in the 1860s and 1870s were, nonetheless, zealously searching for other sumptuous furniture designs. The lofty-sounding designation Renaissance Revival befitted the grandiose furnishings replicating ponderous 1400s, 1500s and 1600s decorative lines.

Carved winged griffins were popular motifs for Renaissance Revival furnishings.

Loomism

Think of Renaissance Revival as Spooky/ Medieval Revival. Gloomy carvings such as cherubs, lion's heads, winged animals and other ponderous motifs once again dominated furniture.

Forsythes' Auctions

Renaissance Revival Trademarks
THE RETURN OF GLOOM

In the mid-1800s, decorating history repeated itself. Once more, interiors grew dim, following the longstanding custom before the Queen Anne and Chippendale styles. Fashion dictated sunless rooms dominated by towering ceilings, dreary dark colors, dark varnished woodwork and tall narrow windows encased in layers of weighty, sun-blocking draperies. Such solemnity created the atmosphere of a mau-

The carved oak griffins flanking the mirror
on this sideboard testify that Renaissance Revival
does indeed look like Medieval Revival.

Forsythes' Auctions

soleum, but for many Victorians, a bleak ambience was the epitome of "House Beautiful" because Gilded Age households regarded Renaissance Revival as the pinnacle of grand taste.

THE RETURN OF WALNUT AND OAK

History repeats itself. Walnut and oak, as had been the case in the early 1700s, were the premier woods. During the heyday of Chippendale, Hepplewhite, Sheraton and Empire, those two timbers had been passed over in favor of mahogany.

Renaissance Revival furniture often had Gothic touches, as you can see in this late 1800s bookcase.

Skinner Auctions, Inc.

This Renaissance Revival desk was made by the Wooten Desk Company of Indianapolis, Ind. It has a patent date of 1874 and opens to reveal many storage areas.

Forsythes' Auctions

Forsythes' Auctions

A pair of restrained Renaissance
Revival walnut bookcases.

However, when designs in the 1870s and 1880s called for spooky Renaissance Revival furniture, those two staples from medieval times came back in full force.

No Daintiness

A glance at any Renaissance Revival example reveals its main trademark: this style made large scale pieces. Most furnishings were originally acquired for rooms with ceilings nearly as towering as medieval banqueting halls. Grandiose sideboards and beds seemed to soar skyward like

Gothic churches and were equally ornate. Decorations included carved flowers, fruit, scrolls and a special motif—a female face.

A Definitive Renaissance Revival Piece
THE SIDEBOARD

Renaissance Revival sideboards were typically at least 6 feet long and 9 feet high. The base contained storage areas with doors, drawers and a marble serving area. Usually an attached framed mirror on top reflected precious gas lighting before the advent of electricity. Trademark motifs were a carved elk or deer head (complete with horns) or a female face reminiscent of the Statue of Liberty.

Two Renaissance Revival Superstars
THE STATUE OF LIBERTY

Such remarkable adornments portraying lovely females graced many Renaissance

This walnut carved stand is a fine example of the Renaissance Revival style.

Victorians were fond of these ornately carved chairs for entranceways.

Forsythes' Auctions

Although this writing or library table looks as if it came from a Florentine palace, it dates from the late 1800s.

Revival pieces and other household items. In the 1870s, George E. Duncan & Son of Pittsburgh, Pa., made glassware in the "Three Faces" pattern. This motif adorning many compotes and goblets bore a striking resemblance to a former Parisian, who in 1886, turned New Yorker. In furniture terms, both the Statue of Liberty and Duncan glass are pure Renaissance Revival. It just makes good antiques sense that the Statue of Liberty falls under this heading. Although the Renaissance Revival style in France is usually called Henri II (in honor of the 1500s monarch), the French versions have the same characteristics. Frédéric August Bertholdi created the statue in France during the height of the Henri II style. This is another illustration of how mastering furniture styles makes dating other antiques a snap.

BERKEY AND GAY WALNUT BED

Factories in Grand Rapids, Michigan, and Cincinnati, Ohio, made stellar Renaissance Revival furnishings. A label displaying Berkey and

A lovely sideboard, circa 1880, with its ornate carving capturing Renaissance Revival's trademarks.

Jackson's International Auctions

Gay of Grand Rapids literally guarantees museum quality. The Public Museum of Grand Rapids displays a Renaissance Revival bed extraordinaire with a provenance from the 100th birthday of the United States. In 1876, the massive Centennial Exposition was held in Philadelphia to glorify the young republic. The very same walnut bed that was once displayed at the exposition is now regally enthroned at the Grand Rapids museum. Because of its height, ornateness and vividly grained burl walnut panels, this masterpiece truly dominates the gallery. Christian G. Carron, the author of *Grand Rapids Furniture*, proudly states that Berkey and Gay won an award at the Philadelphia Exhibition.

Renaissance Revival was mass-produced, quality furniture created for middle- and upper-class markets. A handmade variation of this style emerged in the 1870s and 1880s, and it is fascinating how the comeback of yet another great style of the Victorian era was launched.

Chapter 15

Victorian, Part IV:
The Aesthetic Movement

In the late 20th century, a new term was coined for a subgroup of Renaissance Revival furniture. The elegant tag "Aesthetic Movement" was especially created for handmade Renaissance Revival furniture.

As machinery made more household items in the late 1800s, many artisans were not pleased. The Arts and Crafts Movement emerging during this time demanded more handcraftsmanship for household goods. We'll take a closer look at this traditonal craftsmanship in upcoming chapters, but for now, keep in mind that Aesthetic Movement furnishings were handmade examples of Renaissance Revival style.

In the late 1980s, an exhibition at the Metropolitan Museum in New York City really gave the Aesthetic Movement status. "In Pursuit of Beauty" highlighted masterpieces from the 1870s and 1880s created by the renowned decorating firm Herter Brothers of New York, and other American artisans. The displays, although handmade, still bore Renaissance Revival traits, including massiveness, ornateness and, occasionally, spooky carvings.

Jackson's International Auctions

If the lady in this oil painting knew her frame was in the Aesthetic Movement motif, she might have looked happier.

Museum Curators: Antiques Trendsetters

Do you know who really sets antique trends? No, not television, movies or the rich and famous. Articles once deemed only worthy of garage sales can be elevated to "museum quality" status because of these wonderful professionals. Artifacts that

A frame certainly can make a painting, especially if it follows the Aesthetic Movement.

museum curators have specifically chosen for exhibitions become known as "museum quality" and, of course, up go prices. For example, an Aesthetic Movement writing table from the 1880s, which until the 1970s was considered nothing extraordinary, became big league after museum exposure. Because museum endorsement creates trendiness (with inflated prices), suddenly Aesthetic Movement achieved a status equal to Chippendale. Such is the recent history of Herter Brothers and other excellent

The carving of this oak hall bench captures the designs of Aesthetic Movement, giving it quite a Medieval look.

Jackson's International Auctions

Even silver was given the Aesthetic Movement treatment. Both the silver plate caster stand (left) and water pitcher (right) would go perfectly with an Aesthetic Movement sideboard.

Aesthetic Movement artisans.

One of the most enticing displays of Aesthetic Movement furniture is in the Cincinnati Wing at the Cincinnati Art Museum in my beloved hometown. This great hall highlighting furniture crafted in Cincinnati has been the lifetime work of my pal and colleague, Anita J. Ellis, the museum's head curator. The Cincinnati Wing is brimming with wonderful examples of decorative arts produced in Cincinnati since the city's founding in 1788. Silver, Rookwood pottery, paintings and furniture are all there. As you meander into one section of superornate furniture, you know you are looking at Art Carved Furniture, also known as Aesthetic Movement.

The hand-painted designs on these German vases are pure Aesthetic Movement design.

Jackson's International Auctions

Jackson's International Auctions

Although this oak chest looks as if it came from the 1600s, it was made around 1900 in true Aesthetic Movement spirit.

When the Met displayed Aesthetic Movement furniture, I was the antiques columnist for the *Cincinnati Enquirer*. Writing about that exhibit was quite a thrill because the focal point of that exhibit is the show stopper of the Cincinnati Wing. The star is a bed designed by Benn Pitman (1822-1920), the great Cincinnati carver. His wife, Adelaide Nourse Pitman (1859-1893) actually did the carving, and her sister, Elizabeth Nourse (1859-1938) painted the panels. Elizabeth Nourse is a beloved artist of the Queen City, whom I affectionately call "the Mary Cassatt of Cincinnati." Back in the 1980s, I appraised this bedstead when it was donated to the Cincinnati Art Museum. It was a pleasure then and remains so now to gaze on its ornately carved mahogany headboard, whose carved birds are so three-dimensional they seem ready to fly away. If you want to be completely immersed in Aesthetic Movement furniture, visit the Cincinnati Art Museum.

And in the following chapter, as the antiques cliché goes, history was about to repeat itself.

Chapter 16

Centennial: The Return of Duncan Phyfe and Ethan Allen

The 100th anniversary of the signing of the Declaration of Independence was a momentous milestone for the United States. To mark this jubilant occasion, the Centennial Exposition, resembling a World's Fair, was held in Philadelphia, as I touched on in the Renaissance Revival chapter.

The Fervor for "Olde Tyme" Artifacts

The Philadelphia Exhibition of 1876 glorified America's technological advances as well as its history. A colossal crowd-pleaser was the "New England Kitchen." This jam-packed display of Colonial relics aroused a zest for the "Olde Tyme," a then pet name for ancient objects. As a result, throngs of Americans became collecting aficionados, triggering the need for an updated definition for "antique." As I mentioned before, by the early 1900s, "antique" had replaced "curio" as the modern vernacular for old objects.

REPRODUCTIONS

The public's rekindled enthusiasm for the "Olde Tyme," combined with its new zest for antiquing, inspired merchants to move a step backward in decorating styles. Always trying to entice a spend-happy public, manufacturers turned to the "Olde Tyme" styles: Queen Anne, Chippendale, Hepplewhite, Sheraton and Empire. Swanky designations such as "Pilgrim," "Early American," and "authentic reproduction" were coined for the innovative furniture lines in order to appeal to the Victorian sense of status.

Grand Rapids, Michigan, known for curlicue furniture, became a hub for fine reproductions. Berkey and Gay, the firm celebrated for the Renaissance Revival bed in the Grand Rapids museum, also became known for quality renditions of 1700s and early 1800s styles. The John Widdicomb Company, founded in 1897, and Baker Furniture, started in 1903, made first-rate pieces inspired by Chippendale, Hepplewhite and Sheraton. Meanwhile, quality reproductions from the Robert Mitchell Company and Henshaw Furniture, both of Cincinnati, competed against Grand Rapids goods.

WALLACE NUTTING: AN ANTIQUER EXTRAORDINAIRE

Realizing that furniture reproductions were recolonialzing America, Wallace Nutting (1861-1941), recalled his tour of the Centennial Celebration. As a 15-year-old, he marveled at the steam engines on display, but what truly mesmerized him were the Colonial artifacts.

In early adulthood, Nutting was a Congregational minister, but when stress forced him to leave the ministry, he turned to photography. He photographed "Old Tyme" settings resembling those he had seen at the fair. Artistic scenes resplendent with antiques like spinning wheels and lovely ladies in old-fashioned costumes (a savvy touch guaranteeing good sales) became his trademark. By the early 1900s, he had sold more than 5 million photos. Today, his signed hand-tinted photos sell from hundreds of dollars to more than a thousand dollars.

Nutting's success as a photographer motivated him to collect early American furniture and then fabricate "authentic" copies of originals. His quality replicas and photographs were offered through catalogues. The entrepreneur even restored five Colonial buildings in Connecticut and Massachusetts to create the appropriate ambience for his reproductions and photographs.

COLONIAL REVIVAL

The Colonial craze became big business in the United States. Even architects became enthralled with "Old Tyme" touches. Many buildings and residences from the late 1800s and early 1900s captured early American elements now characterized as "Colonial Revival." It's easy to spot these timeless beauties; just look for motifs typical of Colonial Williamsburg, Virginia, such as wooden shutters, half-round windows, painted woodwork and evenly spaced windows.

Even the White House, veteran of many redecorations since the early 1800s, received the "Colonial Revival" touch. The wooden paneling in the State Dining Room was painted in the early 1900s to create a 1790s ambience.

Reproductions from Nutting factories or from Grand Rapids or Cincinnati firms have matured as first-class antiques. These younger antiques have at least one advantage over the more mature masterpieces that inspired them. Unlike earlier cabinetmakers, many Industrial Age firms used some form of labeling. You can usually find this wonderful information (whether stenciled, printed on a paper label, or engraved on a metal plaque) on the back of a piece or on the left or right interior side of a drawer. Wallace Nutting often glued a paper label under the seat of his chairs. Such identification will assist Internet or library research to find all the particulars about a treasure. My two favorite research references are William C. Ketchum, Jr.'s *Marked American Furniture 1640-1940* mentioned earlier and, of course, Christian G. Carron's *Grand Rapids Furniture*.

Centennial

Furniture reproductions dating from the 1870s to 1900 are called "Centennial" in honor of the 1876 Fair. Thankfully, these fine copies, which duplicated the wonderful originals, continued to be made throughout the 20th century. As you now know, pieces made from 1900 to 1920 can be considered antique, while those from the Flapper decade or more recent years are semi-antiques/collectibles.

A genuine Centennial Chippendale-style walnut tea table with bird cage.

Jackson's International Auctions

Sears and Ward catalogues are superb tutors for early 20th century antiques. Golden oak refers to American furniture made from the 1890s to the World War I era. I call these reproductions Empire Revival style. The best examples are round dining tables with carved, hairy animal claw feet that were borrowed from Empire pieces from the early 1800s. As the varnished oak aged, the finish acquired a lovely deep amber tone, giving birth to its charming name. An 1897 Sears catalogue advertised a golden oak hallstand with built-in bench, hooks and mirror for $7.50. Those certainly were the "good old days," because in a shop today, you would probably have to pay from 100 to 200 times its 1897 price!

An early 1900s oak writing table in the manner of Queen Anne, thanks to the cabriole legs.

Du Mouchelle's Auction

The 1930s Sears wish book offered numerous reproductions, and one beauty really caught my attention. A charming maple bedroom suite with four-poster bed, dressing table and chest of drawers was described as an "authentic design of an early American group, faithfully reproduced in every detail...for $24.50."

In the 1930s, the then lofty sum of $25 could not only buy a bedroom suite but also a mahogany secretary desk. Sears heralded this handy piece with bookcase top as "Colonial style, serpentine front, and ball and claw feet." Today, a similar semi-antique Chippendale style desk would cost at least $900 in a shop or mall. Although that isn't small change, a 1700s version could cost more than a fancy car.

An early 1900s walnut candlestick stand capturing Queen Anne design trademarks, including pad feet and bird cage.

Jackson's International Auctions

"OF THE PERIOD" VERSUS CENTENNIAL

How can we tell the difference between a Centennial chair and "one of the period" (meaning an original)? It's easy if you follow my Sensual Approach to Learning. Furniture makers manufacturing Centennial pieces often sacrificed the integrity of the 1700s originals in order to please the

Forsythes' Auctions

This walnut 1915 cabinet was made to look very Medieval.

Victorian preference for overstatement. Thus, copies lacked the balance and simplicity of earlier styles.

Centennial pieces were often flamboyantly decorated. Two particularly flashy accoutrements practically shout "reproduction." Remember, this was "The Gilded Age," as Mr. Twain so accurately put it, which means gold abounded even on pieces duplicating 1700s masterpieces. Apparently, to the Victorian eye, adding gold leaf to a Sheraton or Queen Anne piece was essential.

If I dared to modify the title of Mr. Twain's master novel, I would change it to *The Gilded and Mother-of-Pearl Age*. Mother-of-pearl decoration clearly indicates a Centennial origin and comes in a close second to gilding as the favorite Victorian trimming. The lining from oyster shells was used to decorate everything from ballroom chairs to handles on silver flatware. Even great firms such as Berkey and Gay, and Robert Mitchell added mother-of-pearl flourishes to their reproductions. Chair backs were commonly encrusted. Certainly Mr. Chippendale would never have approved, but Victorians adored such lavishness. By 1915, mother-of-pearl and gilding became as outdated as fainting couches and velvet draperies, two other favorites of the Victorian era. Starting in the 1920s, reproductions would never again use such lavish touches for 1700s replicas.

More splashy traits distinguish Centennial from earlier pieces. In keeping with the Victorian's love for soaring heights so evident in homes with high ceilings, reproduction chair backs were often taller than Mr. Chippendale's. Another easy-to-spot trait is found on the feet of chairs. Ball-and-claw feet on a period Chippendale chair are carved from a solid piece of wood. However, on Centennial, Flapper, Depression and Eisenhower-era versions, the feet are constructed from several thin pieces of wood that are glued together, indicating machine carving.

These 10 oak dining chairs with ball-and-claw feet are flamboyant Centennial reproductions mixing Queen Anne (splats) and Chippendale (claw feet). The claw feet bear very little resemblance to Chippendale originals.

THE RETURN OF DUNCAN PHYFE AND ETHAN ALLEN

As a marketing gimmick, manufacturers added clout to reproductions by borrowing names of highly regarded Americans from the "Old Days."

In the 1930s, Duncan Phyfe (1768-1854) became an even more celebrated household name than during his lifetime. The Scotsman, who worked in Manhattan from 1792 to 1847, was highly venerated for his choice Hepplewhite, Sheraton and mahogany pieces. (Today you can see his incredible artistry by viewing one of his sofas displayed in the State Diplomatic Rooms in Washington D.C.)

By the 1930s and the 1940s, Sheraton-style mahogany reproductions of dining room tables and round end tables with brass-capped claw feet were in homes all across America. Many manufacturers crafted these timeless beauties, but rarely did they apply the correct name of "Sheraton." Rather, they labeled their work as "Duncan Phyfe" style, an intentional misnomer to boost sales. Although Phyfe crafted Sheraton-style pieces, he never originated any design. Nevertheless, furniture manufacturers chose to name their reproductions after the New Yorker rather than after Mr. Sheraton. No doubt advertising executives thought that touting a former Scotsman-turned-Yankee would be more appealing to American consumers than promoting a British designer. Ah, the power of Madison Avenue! Thus, the name Duncan Phyfe is forever associated with 1930s and 1940s copies of 1800-Sheraton designs.

Today the name Ethan Allen conjures up thoughts of cozy wing chairs, but once upon a time, the name was associated with patriotism. Mr. Allen (1738-1789) was not a cabinetmaker, but rather a heroic Revolutionary War soldier who fought to make Vermont a state of the Union. In 1936, the Bauritter Company cleverly "borrowed" the legend's name for its furniture line, which proved a hugely profitable strategy. Eighteen years later, the Ethan Allen firm had sold over a million pieces and, to mark the event, it gave a maple chest of drawers to President Eisenhower.

In the next chapter, you will encounter the last great style of the 1800s.

Chapter 17
Art Nouveau, Part I: Tea and Waltzes at the Ritz

In 1898, during the final years of Queen Victoria's rule, the French-man Cesar Ritz (1850-1918) opened the most luxurious inn the world had ever seen. Almost overnight, the Hotel Ritz in Paris became syn-onymous with opulence and was so successful that, in 1905, Mr. Ritz opened his second hotel in London.

"Tea at the Ritz," became an afternoon ritual for trendy Londoners, while Parisians enjoyed a similar tradition with champagne. Before long, the term "ritzy," became the early 1900s vernacular for "upscale" or "high-end." Irving Berlin made the hotels legendary with his 1929 hit song "Putting on the Ritz," whose title also became the name of a 1930 Hollywood movie. While the blue stocking set waltzed and

Treadway Toomey Galleries

Raoul Larche captured French dancer Lois Fuller in bronze around 1900. Consider the swirling motif of this incredible figurine as a definitive example of Art Nouveau.

Jackson's International Auctions

This 1910 bedroom suite from France had a wall unit with a mounted bronze plaque of mother and child, displaying Art Nouveau's lavishness.

Jackson's International Auctions

drank tea and champagne at the Paris and London hotels, Art Nouveau emerged and became identified with the lavishness of those fabled days.

"Ritzy" certainly describes the sumptuousness of early Art Nouveau artifacts. The disciples of this style, like the Arts and Crafts crowd, venerated handcraftsmanship and frowned on machine production. Just as a high tea at the Ritz was not meant for the masses, the same was true for most early Art Nouveau objects.

"Art Nouveau" in French means "modern art." The movement started in the 1880s in France, where handcraftsmanship remained highly respected even during the halcyon days of the Industrial Revolution. In the 1890s, the style arrived in the United States thanks to two world fairs and remained the height of chic for the carriage trade until World War I.

The Italian artist Vittorio Caradossi (b. 1861) carved this Art Nouveau beauty entitled "Nymph" around 1900.

Art Nouveau/Modern Art Trademarks

FLOWING LINES

Art Nouveau not only shares Rococo Revival's ornateness but several other traits as well, including cabriole legs, shells and floral designs. Nevertheless, Art Nouveau artifacts presented these motifs from a slightly different perspective. The movement's most striking characteristic is its flowing look. Art Nouveau can be visualized by imagining a Rococo Revival sofa made from cake and decorated with icing. The sun melts the rose decorations and cabriole legs and, ultimately, the overall shape of the settee, giving it a flowing look. Thus, this style has no sharp edges and is even more flamboyant than earlier Rococo Revival.

Loomism

"Flow" rhymes with "Nouveau." This cue keeps us from getting this style confused with Art Deco, a later design.

FLORAL DESIGNS

Art Nouveau was a 1900s garden of delicate lilies, roses, morning glories and tulips that adorned stained glass, silver, furniture, lamps, subway entrances and a department store. Art Nouveau's intricate and ornate designs were best captured by handcraftsmanship, since factory production could not yet duplicate such opulence.

The Impact of World Fairs

The Universal Exposition of 1889 delightfully transformed Paris. The symbol of the fair, the Eiffel Tower, was controversial because of its height and "bare-bones" design. In the days when ornateness was the norm for buildings and home décor, its exposed steel framework was considered too austere. At 984 feet tall, this forerunner to the modern skyscraper was the highest manmade structure in the world. Could anyone now imagine Paris without this famous landmark? The handcrafted objects displayed at the exhibitions eventually influenced many

Skinner Auctions, Inc.

This 1899 print by Peter Behrens, appropriately entitled "The Kiss," demonstrates the "swirliness" of Art Nouveau.

These European gilded metal candelabrums, circa 1900, are pure Art Nouveau fantasy and catered to the Victorian zest for gold decorations.

Jackson's International Auctions

Victorians loved to place these Art Nouveau metal lamps at the foot of staircases, so naturally, over time, they became known as "newel post lamps."

Early Auction Company

French objects and buildings in that era. Furthermore, foreigners brought home the designs seen at the fairs, giving Art Nouveau a global impact.

In 1895, following Art Nouveau's triumph at the 1889 Fair, the German art dealer Samuel Bing (1838-1905), opened a Parisian boutique. His store offered glass, jewelry, posters and other stylish marvels, with ritzy price tags, of course.

The store did so well that at the following Parisian fair, the Universal Exposition of 1900, Bing displayed more Art Nouveau examples, from chairs to glass shades especially created to sheathe the recently invented electric light bulb. Today in the Museé d'Orsay, near the site of the fair, you can actually see some of these superb antiques.

Tiffany

Concerning Art Nouveau and light bulbs, one antiques legend goes to the head of the class. American Louis Comfort Tiffany (1848-1933) was to Art Nouveau what Chippendale was to English furniture. In 1834, Louis's father, Charles L. (d. 1902), founded the swanky jewelry establishment Tiffany and Company in New York City. As a young man, Tiffany did his Grand Tour of Europe as Robert Adam had the previous century. In Ravenna, Italy, he studied early Christian mosaics, which were religious pictures created from small pieces of stone, marble or glass set in mortar. Another equally seductive learning session occurred in France at the Gothic cathedral of Chartres so fêted for stained glass windows.

An early 1900s stained and leaded glass table lamp, which was more affordable than the high-end Tiffany version. Today, this "Pansy" lamp stands on its own artistic merit.

Skinner Auctions, Inc.

The stained glass windows Tiffany observed in Europe were crafted by painting powdered colored glass onto the surface of clear areas. Tiffany was fascinated with the artwork and wanted to replicate its beauty, but with his own style and technique. His novel technique for creating stained glass windows was adapted from the mosaics he had studied in Italy. He used solidly colored pieces of glass to create motifs, rather than painting on the surface of clear glass. In a window with a floral window scene, for example, he used strips of lead to join green leaf-shaped and red petal-shaped pieces of glass to form a mosaic picture. For creating human hands and faces, however, Tiffany relied on the traditional painting method. In his 1900 masterpiece, "The Four Seasons," various floral blossoms vividly capture the times of the year.

The sun's rays streaming through Tiffany windows were magically luminous, especially when placed on stair landings or on front entrances. As a true Arts and Crafts advocate, Mr. Tiffany loathed how the Industrial Revolution polluted the landscape. Mr. Tiffany brought a whole new meaning to the phrase "seeing the world through rose-colored glass." His colorful and decorative windows enhanced the

Mr. Tiffany made stained glass fashionable. This handsome unsigned example was inspired by Mr. Art Nouveau, but was less costly.

A beautiful example of Mr. Tiffany's genius, this Poinsettia table lamp dates from the early 1900s.

scenery by hiding the ugliness outdoors.

Tiffany's windows brought him enormous success, and the artist would forever be linked with them. "Tiffany" has become a generic term like Morris chairs, which comes from the name of the Arts and Crafts star William Morris. Any chair with a reclining back seems to be called a Morris chair, just as any stained glass lamp or window is called a Tiffany! People say they have a Tiffany window whether crafted by his studio or a competitor. Tiffany shrewdly signed his pieces, which makes it a snap to identify and authenticate his work. His dream home, Laurelton Hall, on Long Island in New York, housed breathtaking Art Nouveau masterpieces including furniture, windows and one special artifact that brought him even greater prominence.

Tiffany turned his creative genius to the then high-tech wonder of electricity by creating Art Nouveau lighting fixtures. A Tiffany lamp usually had a dark-green bronze or ceramic base resembling a tree branch and a mushroom-shaped stained glass shade that softened and beautified the harsh glare of a light bulb. The lampshades typically portrayed flowers such as chrysanthemums, poppies and peonies. Through his artistic touch, Tiffany made this high-tech wonder more attuned to a home's décor, revealing he improved inside panoramas, too. This union of art and science first started in the Art Nouveau pe-

Another popular motif for Art Nouveau stained glass windows was known as "Grapes Hanging from Leaf and Vine."

The "Leaf and Vine" design was very popular for Art Nouveau stained glass windows.

Tiffany Studios crafted this seven-piece desk set in the "Grapevine" pattern. It's made from bronze doré, or gilded bronze, which you learned about in the Empire chapter.

Jackson's International Auctions

A 12-inch high Tiffany Favrile Floriform glass, circa 1908, beautifully captures Art Nouveau.

riod and really blossomed in a style that developed in the 1920s and 1930s.

A Tiffany bronze lamp read "Tiffany Studios" or "Tiffany Furnaces," along with a number on its base. Glass lamp shades, besides being numbered, were marked either "LCT" for Louis Comfort Tiffany or "Favrile," referring to the glass line. The ritzy status of Tiffany endures, since in recent years some have sold for about $200,000! In the early 1900s, the average lamp cost about $110, which for those days was a great deal of money. To illustrate the buying power of a dollar back then, my gram often told me that five cents bought a beer plus a free lunch at a pub!

Tiffany's Favrile line was a special hand-blown glass made by adding a secret formula of chemicals to molten glass to create an iridescent quality. The flowing and almost lighter-than-air Favrile resembles freshly picked blossoms. Favrile brings up an interesting point about antiques and worth. We often assume that value corresponds directly with age, but often that's not the case. Tiffany vases can sell for $8,000 at auction, while a Roman glass piece, almost 2,000 years older, usually goes for a tenth of the younger Tiffany.

L.C.T. certainly lived and died a totally Art Nouveau lifestyle. His death wish was granted, as befitting an Art Nouveau legend, by being buried under 300 carnations in his favorite color—pink.

Gallé

Emile Gallé (1846-1904), whom I affectionately called "the French Tiffany," was another Art Nouveau superstar. Naturally, the French would suggest that Tiffany is "the American Gallé." No problem, because both are gods in any antiquer's bible.

Gallé's sensuous glass vases used Art Nouveau's flowing designs. A metal mold was made from a model created from flexible wax. Molten glass was poured into the form, and when cooled, an Art Nouveau tour de force emerged.

Silver, like glass, adapted brilliantly to Art Nouveau's curving lines. In the 1890s and early 1900s, Art Nouveau motifs graced some of the loveliest flatware ever to garnish a dining table. Art Nouveau cutlery was often bedecked with floral motifs such as morning glories entwining a teaspoon's handle. American silver firms crafted glorious Art Nouveau patterns such as "Peony" (Wallace, 1906), "The Five Flowers" (Reed and Barton, 1900) and "Imperial Chrysanthemum" (Gorham, 1894). Notice that in true Art Nouveau fashion, names centered on flowers.

Art Nouveau superstar Emile Gallé designed this bedroom suite circa 1890.

Jackson's International Auctions

Grueby, Newcomb and Rookwood: Art Potteries Extraordinaire

The Paris World Fairs of 1889 and 1900, besides establishing Art Nouveau, also propelled two American potteries into the artistic limelight. Both Grueby and Rookwood won gold medals for ceramic pieces emblazoned with Art Nouveau motifs. Newcomb Pottery was another highly esteemed Arts and Crafts pottery and, like Rookwood and Grueby, fashioned pieces by hand. All three potteries achieved sinuous ceramic Art Nouveau wonders thanks to clay's plasticity.

Grueby, Newcomb and Rookwood, unlike English Wedgwood and Copeland Spode, were oriented more toward creativity than profit. Rookwood, founded in Cincinnati in 1880 by Maria Longworth Nichols, was known for innovative Art Nouveau pieces but, sadly, closed in 1960. Mrs. Nichols would be amazed to learn that a vase by Kataro Shiraydomani, her premier artist, whom I call the "Greta Garbo" of Rookwood, due to his stellar reputation, sold at auction for $350,750 in 2004.

Loomism

Early Art Nouveau antiques fall under the heading I call Art Nouveau I, the era of tea, champagne and waltzes at the Hotels Ritz.

Newcomb College Pottery was established in 1895, and like the other two ceramicists, used stalwart Art Nouveau motifs including wisteria, magnolias and palm trees. Most pieces dating before 1920 were one-of-a-kind. Newcomb closed in 1930 because of the Depression but remains ever venerated by museum curators and high-end collectors.

In 1894, Bostonian William H. Grueby (1867-1925) opened Grueby Pottery, and right from the beginning, the individually decorated pieces were greatly admired. Even the great Tiffany ordered Grueby ceramic pieces for the lamp bases that would vaunt his stunning shades. That's quite an endorsement! A Ruth Erikson vase cost about $50 in the 1890s, but today sells for thousands. Unfortunately, Grueby went bankrupt in 1908, a sad fate shared by many art potteries.

Silver, ceramics and glass swiftly adapted well to the flowing designs of Art Nouveau, but wood demanded even more artistic ingenuity. Emile Gallé magnificently captured Art Nouveau's cascading designs in chairs, tables and beds, as well as in glass. How startling that Gallé's graceful furniture displayed at the Museé d'Orsay came from rigid trees.

Majorelle

A contemporary of Gallé and Tiffany, Louis Majorelle (1859-1926) is another Art Nouveau luminary. The Frenchman created beds with headboards in the shape of flower petals, and chairs resembling oversized lily blossoms.

Factory renditions of mainstay styles of the Victorian era—Eastlake, Renaissance Revival and Rococo Revival—suited middle-class budgets. Ornate Art Nouveau artifacts, on the other hand, were practically impossible to mass produce. How could machines possibly duplicate Majorelle's chairs resembling lilies? So Art Nouveau furnishings remained mostly handcrafted, with prices far too high for folks living in bungalows and farmhouses all across America.

Art Nouveau I artifacts were crafted by hand, and today, as genuine antiques, are either in museums or belong to the moneyed. Visit a museum to see examples of these beautiful works on display.

By the early 1900s, some American manufacturers finally learned how to mass produce goods with Art Nouveau flourishes. In the next chapter, we'll explore these Art Nouveau goods that are accessible to the masses.

Jackson's International Auctions

A Daum vase made in France around 1910 is a stellar example of Art Nouveau.

Chapter 18

Art Nouveau, Part II: Masterpieces for the Common Man

In the previous chapter, I suggested that you visit museums to savor out-of-this-world Art Nouveau works of art. Now you're about to become familiar with Art Nouveau antiques that our recent ancestors chose for their homes. Even to this day, such Main Street finery from the early 1900s is within our reach. But first, we'll rendezvous with what I consider to be the greatest Art Nouveau masterpiece in the world. No museum ropes will hinder you from touching to your heart's content the graceful swirling Art Nouveau embellishments. No admission fee is charged, and in fact, entry is greatly solicited. You are probably assuming that this incomparable Art Nouveau masterwork is in Paris, London or New York, but guess again. This landmark is located in the very heart of Chicago a few blocks west of Lake Michigan at the corner of State and Madison Streets.

Architecture
CARSON'S
Paris and London have the illustrious Ritz Hotels discussed in the last chapter, but Chicagoans cherish the magnificent Carson, Pirie, Scott Building. The department store designed by Louis Henry Sullivan (1856-1924) became the "Mona Lisa" of his career. Just as that celebrated painting guaranteed legendary status to Leonardo da Vinci, Carson's, as Chicago residents fondly say, secured the same everlasting eminence for Mr. Sullivan. Showing Yankee ingenuity, he mingled ornate French Art Nouveau with the recently invented American skyscraper. Even a century later, the results are still sensational.

Carson, Pirie, Scott and Company was established in the mid-

1800s, (the same era as other department stores discussed earlier), but its new building was erected between 1899 and 1904, approximately the same time as the Paris and London Ritz Hotels. The Sullivan facade in the spirit of Gallé, Majorelle and Tiffany brought (and thankfully still does) Art Nouveau's splendor to the many shoppers on State Street.

Sullivan designed a high-tech building whose skeletal support system dictated its outward appearance. Walls no longer had to be immensely thick because hidden steel beams supported the weight. This technology allowed thinner walls with many large windows to let in light and air.

In the early 1900s, Carson's seemed ultra modern, and perhaps even a touch sterile when compared to many other Chicago landmarks. Those were the days when most buildings were as ornate as Renaissance Revival sideboards.

The outside of Carson's was veneered with terra cotta, which was then the most up-to-date method in construction. Terra cotta is the same baked earth used in clay pots, but the terra cotta tiles used for Carson's also had a glazed (glass-like) surface to make it weatherproof.

Sullivan's technique for adding stylish panache to what could have been a very bland facade reveals his genius. Art Nouveau iron ornamentation was applied to the terra cotta on the lower floors within easy view of shoppers. Sullivan's stylish embellishments softened the austere lines of the 12-story building much the same way dribbling sand removes the sharp edges of a beach castle.

In the 21st century, all Chicago exalts Carson's, and it seems Parisians share that admiration. A few years back, when my family and I were in the book department at Marshall Field's (Carson's friendly competitor located a block north on State), some French visitors were asking in broken English for books about Chicago landmarks. Always trying to be the goodwill ambassador in Franco-American relations, I helped in my B- French. The charming Parisians were utterly thrilled with Chicago buildings, and of course, Carson's was the headliner. When I suggested they visit the Art Institute of Chicago, which I described as "the Louvre of the United States," they passed, saying they had limited time and did not want to miss a single superb building.

I bet those Parisians felt transported to their hometown as they entered Carson's rounded mahogany-encased lobby. Certainly the Sullivan ironwork recalled Parisian landmarks. Early 1900s Metro entrances designed by Art Nouveau superstar Louis Majorelle have that same sinuous Art Nouveau exquisiteness.

OTHER FABULOUS BUILDINGS

The next time you're in the Windy City, continue your antiques learning adventure by exploring Chicago's pioneer skyscrapers. The Chicago Architecture Association presents first-class guided tours of area landmarks. (By the way, Mr. Sullivan's name pops up more often during those excursions than that other legendary Chicago architect, Frank Lloyd Wright, who apprenticed under Mr. Sullivan.) Keep in mind that buildings often follow furniture designs. So when you bump into the Rookery Building (1888), a few blocks from Carson's, you can easily see that its ornate facade truly harks back to Renaissance Revival sideboards.

As Carson's celebrated the grand opening of the Sullivan emporium, factory versions of Art Nouveau were finally being produced with some success. Carson's, Macy's, Wanamaker's and other stores sold affordable machine adaptations of Tiffany, Gallé and Majorelle. Today these examples of Art Nouveau II are tempting antiques with uncelestial prices. Following are several that I hope please you.

Carnival Glass

Carnival glass, an Art Nouveau II superstar, captured the shimmering glow of Tiffany. In the early 1900s, factories attempted to duplicate the colors and delicate look of Favrile glass. To connoisseurs, these adaptations failed to completely capture Favrile's iridescent hues and tissue-paper thinness. In their experienced opinion, assembly-line facsimiles looked garish, like carnival prizes. So elitists christened the less affluent version of Tiffany with the disparaging name "Carnival glass," but despite that drawback, the rank and file adored it. The once uncomplimentary designation stuck, and in time the bad buzz turned upbeat. The name "Carnival" became associated with blissful recollections of rides on Ferris wheels and carousels.

Between 1905 and the 1920s, Carnival glass from fruit bowls to vases graced many humble homes all across America and Canada. How I cherish my tall, thin orange vase my mother gave me that belonged to my English/Canadian great-grandmother Taylor. The Dugan, Imperial, Millersburg and McKee glass factories produced myriad examples. Even today many of these genuine antiques can be nabbed for under $200. As your antiques coach always says, buy from reputable retailers because hard-to-detect reproductions have been around since the 1950s.

Silver Plate Flatware

Buying sterling silver flatware with swirling Art Nouveau patterns like "Les Cinq Fleurs" can quickly deplete our budgets. Since most of us were not born with an antique silver spoon in our mouths, silver plate flatware with the same whirling Art Nouveau designs is a wise choice.

Fortunately, old silver plate doesn't maintain value, which makes it affordable, yet it is just as visually appealing as its sterling sister. Why fork out $50 or more for silver when $5 (or less) gets you a plated spoon? The Art Nouveau "Vintage" pattern by Rogers Brothers is equally stunning. And because plated silver tarnishes at the same rate as sterling silver, few (if any) of your guests will be able to distinguish them.

Silver Plate Dresser Sets

Remember how Victorians became enchanted with matching sets of practically everything for their homes? Silver dresser sets in the late 1800s became another favorite. These accoutrements for beautifying milady usually consisted of comb, brush, hand mirror, nail buffer and buttonhooks.

Art Nouveau silver and plated dresser sets quickly adapted to mass production. From all appearances, friendlier-priced plate resembled solid silver and, like plated flatware, cost your relatives much less. These Art Nouveau works adorned numerous 1910 vanities in bungalows and cottages. Reed and Barton, Wallace, Gorham and other factories produced fine sets with motifs following sterling floral patterns like poppies and lilies. Buy unmatched, yet similarly designed plated pieces, and "marry" them. Don't be surprised if you find examples for less than $50.

Ohio Potteries

ROSEVILLE AND WELLER

Those grand Art Nouveau potteries mentioned earlier—Grueby, Newcomb and Rookwood—crafted pottery for the Fifth Avenue, Lake Shore Drive and Nob Hill crowd. Fortunately, less grandiose firms produced goods for Main Street homes. Inspiration came from upscale potteries (a diplomatic way of saying designs were swiped from loftier makers).

These hand-painted porcelain blank ceramics are colorful examples of Art Nouveau dating from 1900.

By the early 1900s, Zanesville, Ohio, near the state capital of Columbus, had become a major pottery center of the United States. "Clay City" was blessed with large high quality clay deposits needed for ceramic production.

Roseville and Weller, two well-known Zanesville factories, replicated the Art Nouveau motifs of Grueby, Newcomb and Rookwood. Only a few decades ago, such pieces were deemed worthy only of garage sales and thrift shops. But today, Roseville and Weller have become statusy staples in antiques shops and malls. Even with higher prestige and heftier prices, Zanesville pieces remain far more affordable than museum favorites Grueby, Newcomb and Rookwood.

In the 1890s, Samuel A. Weller (1851-1925) introduced top-of-the-line "Louwelsea" which appeared to be an out-and-out imitation of Rookwood. Weller created reasonably priced wares capturing the beauty of Art Nouveau, but unfortunately the factory closed in 1949. Roseville, another "Clay City" pottery, was very successful and produced lovely pieces that with a little luck can still be found in shops and malls in the $200 to $300 range. Weller's name was incised on wares, and Roseville was marked "Rozanne, R.P. Co." Roseville met the same fate as sister potteries when it closed in 1954.

HUTSCHENREUTHER, ARNFELDT AND LENOX

By the late 1900s, Europeans had perfected mass-production of affordable quality china, resulting in a pleasurable pastime for artists who decorated them. The china firms Hutschenreuther in Germany, Arnfeldt in France, and Lenox in America produced unadorned ceramics called "porcelain blank." These pieces left the factory blank—totally plain and undecorated. While Tiffany was crafting his works of art, recreational china painters repeated Art Nouveau flourishes on porcelain blank. The hand-painted wares were then baked in a kiln to create a glass-like coating to protect decorations. Glazing hand-decorated porcelain blank was how Maria Longworth Nichols established Rookwood Pottery.

One of the most appealing aspects about porcelain blank has to do with verification. As an appraiser, I must frankly tell you that it is not always possible to know the exact age of antiques. That's when the term "circa," meaning "approximately," is used. But "circa" is rarely needed to describe porcelain blank, because the talented artists wisely signed and dated their handiwork. One of my favorite Christmas decorations is a plate from Limoges, France, that was decorated in the United States. On the back the artist wrote "Xmas 1891 from a friend." Today bowls, teacups and other ceramic pieces complete with Art Nouveau trimmings can be yours for less than you ever dreamed. How about $10 for a dinner plate!

Furniture

Art Nouveau furniture was rarely mass produced because machines could not carve meandering decorations in wood. Such curvy furniture required hand-craftsmanship, which kept prices out of reach for most.

You may occasionally stumble on a factory piece with some Art Nouveau panache. The decoration is usually a flat floral motif, since it was not hand carved, but rather pressed into steamed wood with an embossed metal roller. If you crave Art Nouveau for your home, look for a little curio cabinet about 4 feet

The curvy lines of this mass-produced settee were influenced by Art Nouveau.

Forsythes' Auctions

tall with a series of small shelves resting on curvy legs. These 1910 gems were originally sold through Sears, Roebuck and Montgomery Ward catalogues. Don't pay more than $350.

Another Art Nouveau piece you may consider just happens to be one of my recent purchases. A mahogany sheet music cabinet about 4 feet high practically yelled at me at the Allegan Antiques Show in Michigan. The door has an Art Nouveau musical motif resembling costly hand inlay, but close inspection revealed machine stenciling. The dealer came from metropolitan Chicago, which fed my antiques imagination. Sometimes I envision that my $90 nonmuseum treasure originally came from Carson's around the time Mr. Sullivan finished his masterful endeavor. While no longer holding sheet music, it is perfect for storing office supplies and a pleasure to gaze upon during hectic days at work.

Au Revoir Art Nouveau (But Not for Long)!

As World War I tragically devastated Europe, Art Nouveau was considered an opulent relic from a vanished era. Ironically, Art Nouveau craftsman started the then revolutionary idea of wedding art to technology. Early examples of this union are Tiffany sheathing the naked light bulb with colorful glass, and Sullivan fancifying Carson's. The marvels of machinery in an ever-increasing urban society demanded an art more adaptable to industrialization. The trend that followed Art Nouveau—even more than 80 years after its luminous premiere—remains ever up-to-date.

By the late 1960s, Art Nouveau began its comeback and today is more chic than ever. How extraordinarily grand that for so long the Ritz Hotels in London and Paris, and Carson, Pirie, Scott in Chicago have been safeguarded from destruction or modernization. In the 21st century, these antique landmarks still blaze as eternal Art Nouveau superstars.

Jackson's International Auctions

The lightweight look of this vintage 1900 chair showcases Art Nouveau's stylish lines.

Chapter 19
Arts and Crafts: The Return to Handcraftsmanship

During the final years of Queen Victoria's reign, the Industrial Revolution was generally considered quite wondrous. Nonetheless, some artisans scorned such progress. Handcraftsmanship was practically dying out when the British Arts and Crafts Exhibition Society was created in 1888, giving birth to the Arts and Crafts Movement. This informal alliance of artisans venerating handcraftsmanship brought about the following styles: Aesthetic Movement, Art Nouveau and Craftsman/Mission. This chapter focuses on Craftsmen/Mission, the last style from from the Arts and Crafts Movement.

These various Rookwood Pottery ceramics range from 1880s examples to the charming penguin bookends (lower right hand corner) created in 1934.

This late version of Arts and Crafts dates from circa 1918. The unsigned umbrella stand on the left is from the same era.

Even umbrella stands were given the Arts & Crafts touch in the early 1900s.

Arts and Crafts, Phase I

WILLIAM MORRIS

William Morris (1834-1896), abhorring the Industrial Age, wrote the premier Arts and Crafts manifesto in 1879. In *The Art of the People*, Morris reflected on an "art made by the people, and for the people, as a happiness to the maker and the user." His firm, Morris, Marshall, Faulkner & Co., founded in 1861, became celebrated for high-end handcrafted wallpaper and fabrics, all out of reach for most working folk.

In 1865, years before creating his written proclamation, Morris invented a chair that was even cozier than wing chairs. Modern "La-Z-Boy" recliners are based on his design. The Morris chair was probably an adaptation of a deck chair, adding an adjustable back. In time, an improved model arrived with built-in foot rest that popped out. Imagine the impact of this dandy model during the heyday of Rococo Revival chairs so downright uncomfortable with stiff backs and tiny seats. This innovation now known as the Morris chair made the designer an antiques legend.

Albert Valentien made this unique pitcher for Rookwood in 1883.

An unexpected artistic twist arrived when a shrewd manufacturer pilfered the Morris design. The factory version, so easy to mass produce, was far less costly than high-end handmade Morris originals. Naturally, in the days of user-unfriendly chairs, such seating apparatus became a huge seller. Prototypes of Morris originals were eventually sold in Sears and Wards catalogues. Thanks to the Industrial Revolution, Morris became as honored as the renowned furniture designer of the previous

The vase on the left was crafted by Wilhelmina Post for Grueby Pottery between 1898 and 1907. The flower pot/jardinière on the right is also by Grueby and dates from the same period.

century, Thomas Chippendale. How ironic that the Arts and Crafts spokesman extraordinaire owes his legendary status to the mass production he detested. But look at it this way: the Morris chair maintained interest in its inventor, whose beliefs may have otherwise been forgotten.

Morris and other Arts and Crafts artisans glorified honest construction, quality, durability and little decoration. These traits adapted quite successfully to the Industrial Age.

Arts and Crafts, Phase II

William Morris was the premier artisan of the first stage of the Arts and Crafts Movement. At the turn of the 20th century, this artistic philosophy entered a second phase brought about by Yankee ingenuity. Although machinery took over this stage, craftsmanship still ruled. The goal was to make quality items under the factory system following Arts and Crafts beliefs.

Arts and Crafts was known for large pieces of furniture, such as this massive cabinet. Perhaps it originally held Grueby and Rookwood vases.

GUSTAV STICKLEY

When the Arts and Crafts Movement stormed America, Gustav Stickley (1857-1942) reached his peak. Around 1900, Stickley began producing Craftsman furniture following the Arts and Crafts Movement. Although Craftsman was machine created, Stickley, like Morris, wanted to "make furniture strong, durable, and comfortable, and to base whatever beauty might be attained upon sound structural qualities."

Craftsman furniture was usually oak—undecorated, comfortable and durable. Pieces had a square or rectangular look, along with an honesty of construction revealing structural elements. Mortise and tenon joints, an ancient method for joining wood, were visible, especially on bookcases where top horizontal pieces fitted into the sides. A tenon or tongue of one piece was inserted into the mortise or hole of another.

An oak table made by Charles Limbert of Grand Rapids, Michigan, in the early 1900s.

Then a second, smaller hole was drilled for a peg to be pounded into place to secure both. Although machine produced, such traditional methods recalled handcraftsmanship.

Another strong influence made an impact on Stickley's designs. Stickley loved the understated elegance of Shaker pieces and gave them much credit for inspiration. Stickley was an important influence that helped bring an end to Victorian clutter in the early years of the 20th century. Craftsman pieces had no carvings of gargoyles or fruit, burl walnut panels or any gilt embellishments. Upholstery was never velvet, deemed so proper for Renaissance Revival. Instead, practical and enduring leather was the favored covering.

Skinner Auctions, Inc.

From 1901 to 1913, Stickley published catalogues titled "Craftsman Furniture made by Gustav Stickley," which allowed him to sell directly to the customer. In the furniture-making town of Grand Rapids, Michigan, Stickley exhibited his designs. The catalogues and shows helped promote his name and influenced many Stickley imitators.

Here's Gustav Stickley's early 1900s version of the famous Morris chair.

The Craftsman line became known as the best, but many copied its trademarks. It's similar to how various forms of polo players are used to decorate shirts in an an attempt to mimic the costlier maker. The same happened to Mr. Chippendale back in the mid-1700s.

The name "Craftsman" was coined by Mr. Gustav Stickley, but some clever manufacturer came up with calling equivalent designs "Mission" or "Mission Oak style." Antiquers will often hear these two misleading terms. A story was concocted claiming that the design originated with furniture used in the old Catholic missions before California became a state. This invented name stuck, however, and pieces by Stickley and his imitators are frequently, but

Treadway Toomey Galleries

Gustav Stickley created this library table personifying the Arts and Crafts Movement.

incorrectly, called "Mission." The "Craftsman" designation belongs only to Mr. Stickley.

The most famous Stickley was the oldest of six brothers. Two of his siblings, Leopold and George, quit working for Gustav's firm. In 1900 in Fayetteville, New York, they founded the L. and J. G. Stickley Company. They made "Craftsman" type furniture in the "Mission" style, as well as Morris chairs and Frank Lloyd Wright designs. Gustav never approved of his brothers using veneer on pieces, but in 1916, they bought Gustav's firm and operated it under the name Stickley Manufacturing Company. All three Stickleys are highly collected, but Gustav gets the higher prices at auctions.

ELBERT HUBBARD

Another famous American participant of the Arts and Crafts movement was Elbert Hubbard (1856-1915). After his enlightening visit with Mr. Morris in England, he opened his Roycroft Shop in East Aurora, New York, in 1895. His specialty was "Craftsman or Mission style" furniture, usually of oak, with simple rectangular lines reminiscent of Stickley pieces. From 1905 to 1912, he even made a version of the Morris chair. Inkwells, books printed on handmade paper, and copper items such as bookends and trays came from his shop. Today, furniture by Hubbard is often called "Roycroft" or "Mission," and are highly valued antiques from the Arts and Crafts Movement.

The furniture inspired by the Arts and Crafts Movement is now more fashionable than ever. Gustav Stickley deserves much credit. His early efforts to declutter American homes through his Craftsman furniture was no easy task. After 60-odd years of the "too-much-is-not-enough" decorating mindset of the Victorian era, he was a pioneer of low-key decorating.

Treadway Toomey Galleries

Rocker #407 by Stickley Brothers has the Art & Crafts look.

Chapter 20

Art Deco: A Streamlined Style

Queen Victoria's death in 1901 officially marked the finale of the Victorian era. But grandiose Gilded Age decorating trends lingered until

Skinner Auctions, Inc.

trailblazers in the Flapper decade finally swept away Victorian clutter.

Elsie de Wolfe, a very successful decorator in the early 1900s, loathed Victorian clutter. The New Yorker advocated an "unprecedented restraint" to avoid the "over doneness" of Gilded Age decor. By the 1920s, two stylish transformations arrived that we still enjoy today. The first marked a revived fervor for pre-1840 understated furnishings, and the second gave birth to a style that, even 80 years after its debut, remains perfectly modern.

A magnificently streamlined room divider that is more than 70 years old but looks like it was made last month.

Centennial Emerges as "Authentic Reproduction"

Pioneer Miss de Wolfe, shunning Victorian frills, preferred antique styles such as Queen Anne and Chippendale, with a substantial dose of reproductions. Unlike earlier Centennial copies, 1920s and 1930s editions were more authentic, copying originals line for line and cabriole leg for cabriole leg. No flashy mother-of-pearl, once so prominent on Centennial, was ever incorporated in Flapper reproductions. American firms including Berkey and Gay, Robert Mitchell, Kittinger, Winthrop, and Stickley, created fantastic replicas. The Museum of Grand Rapids, Michigan, highlights fine examples from this era, all examples of the golden age of American furniture manufacturing.

The 1920s and the 1930s witnessed devotees for antiques and

Louis Icart (France, 1888-1950) is one of the outstanding artists of the Art Deco era.

reproductions as well as new-fangled designs. Elsie de Wolfe and followers preferred the tried-and-true from centuries gone by, while a Parisian event fired an artistic revolution. In May 1925, the International Exposition of Decorative Arts displayed never-before-seen artifacts including ceramics, glass, furniture and silver. At the time, these sensations were dubbed "the Modern Style" or "the International Style" because artisans and influences were multinational.

Such designations for this new trend were somewhat confusing and also lacked the dash so needed to capture public attention. As movie stars have known since Nickelodeon days, the power of stylish names should never be underestimated. That flaw ended in 1968 when a Parisian museum exhibiting originals from the 1925 Exposition formulated the charismatic title "Art Deco." An antiques star was reborn.

Loomism

Think "Art UnDeco" to remember Art Deco's low-key decoration.

The gazelle was a popular motif for many Art Deco furnishings such as this 1925 onyx, marble and bronze clock set.

Treadway Toomey Galleries

These French lounge chairs were crafted around 1925.

To create a mental image of Art Deco, visualize 1910 Art Nouveau Gibson Girls with hour-glass figures in flowing white dresses. Now compare Gibson Girls to Miss Art Deco herself, famous 1920s movie star "It" girl, Clara Bow. The premier 1920s Flapper was known for short bobbed hair and knee-length sack dresses.

Art Deco Influences

Several influences molded Art Deco. An essential ideology was borrowed from Art Nouveau. The style of Tiffany, Gallé and Majorelle tried to bring art to one and all, but sadly, only millionaires could afford such lavishness. In the 1930s, Art Deco finally succeeded so grandly at fulfilling Art Nouveau's goal of bringing art to the masses.

Treadway Toomey Galleries

CUBIST ARTISTS

Geometric motifs, which were Art Deco trademarks, evolved from Cubist artists. In the early 1900s, painters living in Paris created pictures dominated by angular lines. Pablo Picasso (1881-1974), in "Les Demoiselles d'Avignon," geometrically diagrammed Barcelona call girls from various angles. Cubist geometric shapes eventually embellished Art Deco household goods, skyscrapers and, not one, but two world fairs.

Charles Turzak's "Medley of Rectangles" captures Art Deco's colors and geometrical shapes.

BALLET RUSSE

On May 19, 1909, during Cubism's zenith, the Russian Ballet performed "Les Sylphides" in Paris. The flamboyant costumes shocked audiences, but practically overnight the show-stopping colors radically affected home decor. Fainter colors, so esteemed in Art Nouveau and Rococo Revival, gave way to pulsating greens, reds, oranges, and blues—all Ballet Russe inspired.

EGYPT

Egyptian touches, so trendy in the early 1800s during the French Empire, once again became the rage when the tomb of Pharaoh Tutankhamen was discovered in 1922. Mummified King Tut, (from 353 B.C.), rivaled Cubist paintings and Ballet Russe when it came to inspiring designs. Egyptian motifs such as triangularly shaped palm trees and pyramids influenced everything from wall-to-wall carpeting to the swanky new "Graumann's Egyptian Theatre" in Los Angeles. The record-breaking museum tour of King Tut's artifacts in the late 1970s refueled the fanfare for Art Deco.

Architects

FRANK LLOYD WRIGHT

Frank Lloyd Wright (1869-1959), an inventive architect second-to-none, severed all links with past architectural styles. Wright was to architecture what designer Coco Chanel had been to women's fashions. Chanel freed women from the bustles and corsets of Victorian days with the slender, streamlined, non-hourglass-shaped Clara Bow Flapper style. Wright in 1904 designed the Larkin Building in Buffalo, New York, complete with central air conditioning, double paned glass windows and steel office furniture. The office building was "streamlined," meaning you would never see a stone gargoyle or any other type of unnecessary ornamentation. Streamlining summarizes Wright's contribution to Art Deco architecture.

Loomism

To understand streamlining, think of the dieting we endure to rid our bodies of unwanted fat.

WALTER GROPIUS AND THE BAUHAUS SCHOOL

Another Art Deco superstar and Wright disciple, Walter Gropius (1893-1969), founded the Bauhaus School in Weimar, Germany, in 1919. "High-tech" building materials such as steel, concrete, and glass,

Magnificent pieces made by two stars of the Art Deco era. The table was designed by Mies van der Rohe, circa 1930. The top is wood painted black, resting on metal legs. Around the same time, Marcel Breuer designed the chair, which features chromium-plated steel and black paint with canvas seat and back. Both designs are timeless.

Skinner Auctions, Inc.

carrying Bauhaus designs were used rather than old-fashioned wood.

The Breuer Chair

A Bauhaus fan, Marcel Breuer (1902-1981), in 1925 patterned a chair with tubular chromium-plated front legs. The design resembled Wright's office furniture created for the Larkin Building. The timeless and so severely elegant Breuer chair has never gone out of style and is now approaching genuine antique status.

A mixture of influences, the Exposition of 1925 was held near the Eiffel Tower. Showcasing revolutionary designs, Art Deco items from the fair were handmade and expensive. The goods displayed there represent the first era of Art Deco.

Lalique Glass

Of all the breathtaking Art Deco items highlighted, Lalique glass from France is probably the best known. It makes us envision Clara Bow dabbing Coty perfume from Lalique bottles before doing the Charleston. Rene Lalique (1860-1945), became the most celebrated Art Deco glass maker.

Following Art Deco's stellar unveiling at the Exhibition of Decorative Arts, the French clamored for the Jazzy style. In just a few years, Art Deco had practically taken over Paris, from the facades of recently constructed buildings to furnishings sold at the famous Parisian store, Au Printemps, on the Boulevard Haussmann. But when the modern style conquered America, main street was never the same again.

Chapter 21

Art Deco Transforms Main Street

The Ile de France

In 1927, the French ocean liner *Ile de France* created an artistic sensation when it docked in New York harbor. The floating Art Deco palace introduced geometrically designed and colorful furnishings to trend-conscious New Yorkers.

Manhattan stores soon realized the potential of the bewitching new design that had just arrived from France. The posh emporium Saks Fifth Avenue became an Art Deco showcase displaying this new French style. Soon Art Deco, raccoon coats and bobbed hair became the rage for the Park Avenue crowd.

Shortly after Art Deco seduced New Yorkers, the stock market crash of 1929 devastated the finances of all strata of American society. As food lines formed from New York to California, Art Deco entered its second and truly unparalleled epoch. The geometric designs of Lalique, Ruhlman and others were easily tailored to mass production and middle-American tastes on tight Depression budgets.

How Art Deco finery was so needed during those difficult years! During the 1930s, almost a quarter of the American labor force was unemployed, and the madman Hitler loomed in Europe. While all that stormed, Art Deco economically and ever so smartly transformed homes that surprisingly, even as late as the 1930s, still slumbered in Victorian curlicue.

Loomism

Regard Art Deco as Main Street Deco because in the 1930s, America was "Decoized" from East to West and North to South.

The Chicago World's Fair of 1933

Art Deco at two world fairs, the first in Chicago and the second in New York, brought cheer to an anxious world. The "Century of Prog-

Skinner Auctions, Inc.

The Widdicomb Company of Grand Rapids manufactured this curved mahogany chest of drawers around the time of the two American world fairs.

ress" celebrating Chicago's Centennial, opened on May 27, 1933. This incredible feat, financed entirely without federal funds, occurred along the Lake Michigan shore just south of downtown Chicago, near the present site of McCormick Place.

The fair's pavilions were decorated in gleeful Art Deco colors, first seen at the 1909 Ballet Russe. Fairgoers must have been invigorated by such a cheerful environment of yellows, reds and oranges heralding a better life, thanks to modern technology. The message was "There is still optimism and beauty in this world, and we shall make it!" How fondly my antiquer Aunt Panny reminisced about this marvelous attraction. Even as a mature adult, her enthusiasm was as fervent as if she had just been there. Such was the uplifting effect of this celebration.

The Sky Ride transporting passengers in cars suspended over the exhibition was a big hit. The pulsating fairgrounds and nearby skyscrapers such as the Wrigley Building in Chicago's Loop offered out-of-this-world views. Another presentation that science could never rival and Aunt Panny would never mention attracted record throngs. We so often regard the old days as entirely wholesome, but the Chicago Fair suggested otherwise. With only fans separating Sally Rand from enthralled audiences, the legendary dancer presented a rather risqué performance. With her costume ever so streamlined, the lady received a Rococo salary of $3,000 per week, while the average secretary made about $20. From time to time, the fantastic Chicago Historical So-

Forsythes' Auctions

This Art Deco five-cent slot machine was displayed at the 1933 Chicago Fair.

This colorful illustration captures less than half of the enormous Chicago World's Fair.

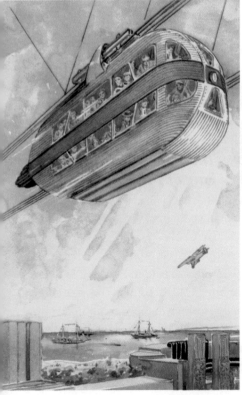

The Travel and Transport Building at the Chicago Fair was billed as "larger than the dome of Saint Peter's [in Rome] or that of the Capitol in Washington." Notice the Art Deco colors.

Here's a view of the "Sky Ride" at the Chicago World's Fair.

Medieval Paris came to life in one of the many national pavilions at the Chicago World's Fair.

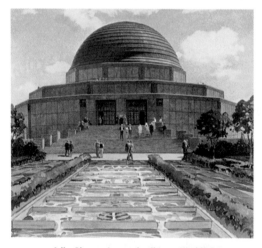

Adler Planetarium at the Chicago World's Fair gave visitors a fantastic look at the heavens.

ciety displays those celebrated and rather transparent fans, along with a movie of the actual ritual. Little was left to the imagination, revealing that by 1933 Puritanism was on the wane and that Miss Rand was a bottled blonde.

The New York World's Fair of 1939

Six years later, Art Deco triumphed once again at the New York World's Fair. The World of Tomorrow opened on April 30, 1939, on the eve of World War II. The huge event was held in Flushing Meadows in Queens, a borough of New York City. Ten thousand trees and a million tulip bulbs transformed a former dump into an enchanting verdant area within view of two Art Deco superstars from nearby Manhattan—the Chrysler Building and the Empire State Building.

Compared to Chicago's rather jazzy image presented at the previous fair, the older and eastern New York City chose a rather staid presentation. No flamboyant Art Deco hues, so prominent in the Windy City, decorated "The World of Tomorrow." Elegant and up-lifting white, so striking amidst the landscaped terrain, became the official color for buildings.

Scientific achievement wrapped in Art Deco packaging caught the public's fancy, temporarily erasing fears of falling civilizations. The Exhibition predicted, as the Chicago Fair had five years earlier, a wondrous future produced by technology. The General Motors show "Futurama," created by superstar designer Norman Bel Geddes, attracted 28,000 visitors per day. Another winner was the miniature display of the United States in the year 1960. The exhibit presented 14-lane highways, slum-free cities, and circular skyscrapers looking remarkably like Chicago's 1960s Marina Towers. Even television debuted with a demonstration of RCA sets that bemused fairgoers.

The famous Johnny Weissmuller from the Tarzan movies starred in Billy Rose's water show "Aquacade." Leaving his loincloth behind in Hollywood, Weissmuller wore streamlined, topless swimming trunks that only recently had become acceptable to wear in public. The official robot of the fair, charismatic Electro, competed with Tarzan for ticket sales.

Visitors also patiently waited to see the The Talk of the Town, a village of 15 ultra high-tech homes ranging in price from several thousand dollars to the astronomical price of $20,000.

A Tour of an Art Deco Home

Let's take a fictionalized tour of one model home to show how 1930s Art Deco brought beauty and technology to Americans—at factory prices. The spiffy showplace had two bedrooms, a kitchen, living and dining areas, a utility room, a patio, one-and-a-half baths, and a one-car garage with a brand-new, air-conditioned Nash automobile. Can you believe all this was available in 1939, the very same year that *Gone With Wind* premiered?

The kitchen, the real show stopper, was "a shining example of the machine" as Chicago's Marshall Field's store touted. Steel cabinets circling three walls streamlined kitchen work by creating myriad storage areas and work surfaces. Stainless steel flatware, so popular in Deco days, was stored in one of the numerous easy slide-out drawers. Unlike silver and silver plate, stainless steel cutlery never needed pol-

ishing. The cabinets stored two sets of fabled Art Deco dishes—"American Modern" and "Fiestaware"—which are now highly fashionable semi-antiques.

AMERICAN MODERN CHINA

"American Modern" china, sold at department stores, is to Art Deco what Favrile glass is to Art Nouveau. The brainchild of famous American designer Russel Wright, geometrically shaped pieces could be purchased in colors such as sea foam green, granite gray, chartreuse and others. Mixing colors was in true Deco spirit and created zippy table settings. Wright enjoyed much success as a designer of furniture in the 1930s, but the 1950s would be his heyday.

A talented art student created this beautiful wooden carving in 1934 that captured all the sensuality of Art Deco.

Kitchens like this splendid model from the 1930s were "beauty in the useful."

FIESTAWARE

Another Deco china stalwart, Fiestaware, in happy-go-lucky colors, was the toned-down version of renowned high-end Clarice Cliff china from England. Made by Homer Laughlin in Ohio, sets were sold between 1936 and 1974 at Woolworth's on Main Streets across America. Fiestaware in flashier colors than American Informal was very thick with concentric ring designs. Colors included yellow, red, cobalt blue and the very special Deco hue, turquoise. Fiestaware is once again being made, so be careful when antiquing. The easiest way to spot a recently made piece is to hold new next to old to differentiate the reproduction from the original. (Also check *Warman's Antiques and Collectibles Price Guide* for more tips.)

These lounge chairs by Russel Wright were called "American Modern."

Mr. Art Deco, Russel Wright, designed this maple desk and chair.

The dining area outside the kitchen was part of the great room, which included the living room. Scant furniture was required, since the section was quite small compared to the oversized dining rooms of Victorian manors. A matching china closet and dropleaf table with four to six chairs filled the space. No sideboard was necessary, thanks to the spacious kitchen cabinets. The suite, of course, was decorated in a geometric veneer design in the manner of French Art Deco designer Emile Ruhlman, famous for his geometric inlay of woods on furniture.

The living room was a whopping 14- by 22-foot expanse featuring a fireplace without mantel. In Victorian times, mantels were showoff places for bric-a-brac dust magnets. Deco homes, in true streamlining spirit, were often demantled to reduce clutter and cleaning.

DEPRESSION GLASS

A large pink Depression glass bowl was typically enthroned on the cocktail table. Depression glass was the friendlier-priced Main Street

Clarice Cliff's "Bizarre Ware Pottery" are the definitive example of Art Deco's geometrical designs and gleeful colors.

These chairs with leatherette upholstery and chrome bodies were made in 1935, but look as up-to-date as if crafted last week.

version of Lalique glass. Like Fiestaware, this 1930s stalwart came in a variety of colors and geometric patterns. (More about Depression glass in Chapter 27.) The cocktail table was a novelty from the 1920s. Before Flapper days, living rooms or, more accurately parlors, usually featured a knee-high tea table or parlor table placed in front of sofas or in centers of rooms. During the 1920s, that Victorian tradition ended as cocktail tables, especially invented for serving strong libations, became mainstream. But when Prohibition endeavored to dry up Americans, the term "coffee table" replaced the earlier name. The restored legality of alcohol marked the return of the cocktail table in the 1930s, while the name "coffee table" continued as well.

A smoking stand near the cocktail/coffee table followed the Bauhaus idea of using high-tech products for household items. Henry Dreyfus, inventor of modern telephones, first created the aluminum smoking stand for the incredible Art Deco train Twentieth Century Limited. By the late 1930s, models resembling a pedestal capped by a doughnut-shaped ashtray with spring mechanism for clearing ashes were as widespread in homes as radios. Today health-conscious collectors use these gadgets as plant stands.

WATERFALL

The master bedroom suite manufactured in Grand Rapids, Michigan, included a dresser, mirror, vanity, bench, nightstand and clothes press. A geometrical inlay of dark and light woods called marquetry (mentioned in Chapter 6), was inspired by the Ruhlman designs first seen in Paris. The fronts of chests of drawers often had curved tops, inspiring the name "Waterfall." These huge sellers were fittingly described in 1930s advertising as "streamlined with the simplicity of modern tastes."

A clothes press, a combination mini armoire/wardrobe and chest of drawers, was part of the suite. The dual-purpose piece shortened dressing time because scrambling from dresser to closet was eliminated.

UNDERWEAR

Since bedroom furniture stored clothing, this is an appropriate moment to state how Art Deco modernized unmentionables. Coopers Inc., in true streamlining spirit, turned men's boxer shorts into sleek "jockey" shorts. Today, the firm is appropriately called Jockey. While men's clothing was being streamlined, some figure-control assistance became available for ladies. According to advertisements of the day, "once-overs" hindered "wayward curves while gently persuading your figure to lithe smoothness." In artistic terms, Madison Avenue advertising jargon meant that girdles were "streamliners." Another marvel from Deco days, synthetic nylon invented in 1939 by the Du Pont Chemical Corporation quickly replaced costlier silk for ladies' stockings.

The colorful bathroom is another outstanding example of Art Deco's "beauty in the useful." Pink fixtures, including the sink and bathtub, vividly contrasted with Ruhlman-inspired black and white ceramic wall tiles. The ceramic wall tiles were considered hygienic and, equally important, simple to clean. The wall-mounted commode, (or in good old American English, the toilet) invented by Frank Lloyd Wright some 30 years earlier, made washing the floor a simpler task.

Transitional Versus Art Deco

In the second bedroom, stylistic icons from the 1700s such as Hepplewhite- and Chippendale-style pieces and chintz floral drapes abound-

Skinner Auctions, Inc.

These 1940 pieces made from birch (a light-colored wood similar to pine) came from the Johnson Furniture Company of Grand Rapids.

ed. How did such old-time basics end up in an Art Deco showplace? The dissimilar décor reminds us that in 1939, two decorating choices existed. Many preferred pre-1840 designs, which included antiques and reproductions following Elsie de Wolfe, but others favored Art Deco. Today, mementos in both tastes fall under the heading of semi-antiques/collectibles and, fortunately, plenty of examples still flourish for all of us to enjoy.

When the New York World's Fair closed, Art Deco lost a major star but its dazzle endured. In nearby Manhattan, Art Deco skyscrapers kept the spirit of the fair soaring. In fact, the Chrysler Building and Empire State Building are more seductive Art Deco examples than any found in museum displays.

The Chrysler and Empire State Buildings

In 1930, the 77-story Chrysler Building became the world's tallest, replacing the Woolworth Building as the record holder. William Van Allen designed the edifice, the first manmade structure taller than the 984-foot-high Eiffel Tower. The building's gray and white motif soared into the clouds and in 1939 offered a peachy view of the "Mad Meadow," the fair's official nickname. The headquarters for Chrysler Motors also testified to the achievements of Walter Chrysler, a true American success story.

The Empire State Building remains one the most famous landmarks in the world. This Art Deco icon designed by Shreve, Lamb and Marmon seems rather subdued compared to the more flamboyant Chrysler Building and the older and more curlicue Woolworth

CLAY TONES

The MELLOW SHADES OF ANCIENT POTTERY

The colors of these handsome new JAYSON Shirts and Pajamas possess a rich and lasting beauty like the hand-mixed shades of the classic urns and vases which inspired them. These blend perfectly with the fabrics of suits, or ties, or robes. Clay Tones have an appeal of which you will never tire. The shirts, with regular or *Jaysonized no-starch, no-wilt collars, are $2. The pajamas are $3. Both are now on display at leading retailers, everywhere. If you fail to find Clay Tones by JAYSON...write us and we will direct you.

F. JACOBSON & SONS, INC · 1115 BROADWAY, NEW YORK

*Jaysonized No-Starch . . . No-Wilt Collar Made Under Celanese Patents.

SHIRTS AND PAJAMAS ..by J A Y S O N

E. Jacobson & Sons, better known as Jayson, manufactured shirts for men in the "mellow shades of ancient pottery." These hues were similar to those of Fiestaware.

Building. The monumental skyscraper even starred in the 1933 classic movie *King Kong*. As the doomed ape climbed the building's exterior to reach the 102nd floor, audiences were equally dazzled by heroine Fay Wray in Kong's grasp and the high-tech radiance of the building. If you haven't seen the classic, check Turner Classic Movies for its next showing.

These Art Deco masterpieces outlasting the Great Depression, War World II, and the remodeling fervor of the 1950s and 1960s, teach more about Deco than any book. While new skyscrapers are erected all the time in Manhattan, these grand dames of the skyline still outshine them all.

Jackson's International Auctions

Molded aluminum plaques such as this charming example entitled "Love Birds," graced elevator doors in many Art Deco skyscrapers.

Chapter 22

Lucy and Ricky: The Queen and King of Mid Century

As I keep saying, the definition of antique is constantly changing, and aren't we grateful? This helps keep supplies constantly replenished for future generations, but it also means that trends are continually evolving. Fortunately, doing my radio show, *Keep Antiquing!*, really helps me stay abreast of the constantly evolving world of antiques. At the Atlantique City Antiques Show, I interviewed a charming dealer named Sherry who taught me a lot about semi-antiques/collectibles from the 1950s. Her merchandise no doubt would remind you of Lucy and Ricky's New York apartment in *I Love Lucy*. The booth was full of blond furniture the color of Marilyn Monroe's tresses, as well as oversized table lamps with huge flamboyant shades, mammoth floor lamps and low, long black coffee tables. Just 20 years ago, all these items were strictly garage sale merchandise, but no more. The current price tags of $500 for a china closet and $1,500 for a lamp demonstrate the dramatic rise in status for these goods.

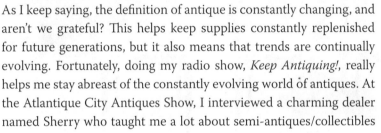

Loomism

The definition of antique is constantly changing, and aren't we grateful?

These semi-antiques/collectibles fall under the heading of the recently coined term "Mid Century." Sitting in Sherry's booth was like being a kid and spending the weekend with Gram in Chicago and, of course, watching Lucy and Ricky. My Flapper grandmother preferred new rather than old. She often tried to sway me from antiques with comments such as, "I like modern things, not old stuff like you do, Frankie." Her apartment was pure Mid Century, except back then her blond dining room suite was called "Danish or Swedish Modern." No doubt Sherry would have been thrilled with Gram's dining set. Come to think of it, Gram had a low, curving sofa just like the one Lucy had for a few seasons before the Ricardos moved to Connecticut. And Gram's sofa was also very similar to one at the Atlantique City show.

This 1950s maple dining suite made by Temple Stuart and Baumeister is pure Mid-Century and reminds me of the set my grandmother had in her Chicago apartment. The china was made by famous Norwegian china maker, Royal Copenhagen.

The furniture in this vintage 1950s setting was designed by Edward Wormley for Dunbar furniture.

During the interview for *Keep Antiquing!*, Sherry taught me something that knocked my socks off. I naturally presumed the fans of Mid Century were 20-something collectors. But to my surprise, Sherry said her buyers are aging baby boomers. I wondered, "Why would anyone who remembers wrought-iron floor lamps from the Lucy decade want to collect them?" My impulse was to say that I didn't like them then, and nothing has changed, but I was on my best professional behavior, which meant keeping mum about my preferences. Sherry taught me that collectors of this era want these mementos because it reminds them of their childhood. What better reason to collect Mid Century! As I always say, buy what you like, so "Bravo" to those baby boomers. Or as my Aunt Panny said, "'Everyone to his or her own taste,' said the little old lady who kissed the cow."

The best news of all is that you already know the design trademarks of Mid Century. Just regard Mid Century as late Art Deco. Keep in mind that the real shaker and mover for Mid Century was

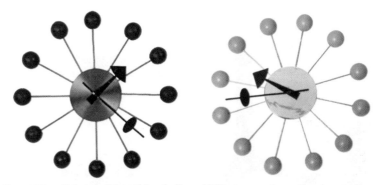

Treadway Toomey Galleries

These 1950s wall clocks by George Nelson for Howard Miller are as modern as if made yesterday.

Russel Wright (who was discussed in the last chapter). The trendsetter achieved much fame during the Deco days of the Chicago and New York world fairs. But remember that the term Mid Century didn't exist in the 1950s. That charming name only came about in the last decade or so.

Mary and Russel Wright

Wright, a native of Lebanon, Ohio, hit the big time when he wrote a best seller. In 1950 Russel and wife, Mary, published the *Guide to Easier Living*. The pair did away with all the pompous lifestyles of previous generations in favor of modern living. They simplified every area of their lives. Russel even dropped the second "l" in his given name in the spirit of streamlining.

Skinner Auctions, Inc.

A 1965 Mid Century version of the Morris chair created in Denmark.

Although Russel Wright wasn't a relative of Frank Lloyd Wright, he was certainly an artistic cousin. He preferred modern open floor plans seen in the architect's work with combined kitchen, dining and living areas so similar to current "great rooms." The couple also preferred lighter-colored woods for furnishings, since dark mahogany seemed too "mu-

Although made around 1951, these "Mid Century" side tables recall Shaker candlestick stands of the mid-1800s.

Skinner Auctions, Inc.

Skinner Auctions, Inc.

Plycraft Chairs manufactured this beauty around 1955, even though it looks quite recent.

Another icon of Mid Century: a George Nelson designed slat bench made by the Herman Miller firm of Zeeland, Michigan.

Jackson's International Auctions

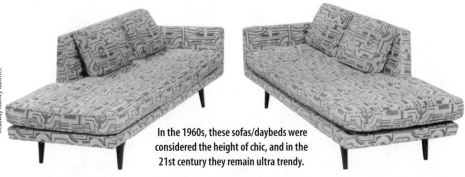

Treadway Toomey Galleries

In the 1960s, these sofas/daybeds were considered the height of chic, and in the 21st century they remain ultra trendy.

seumish" for the style-conscious pair.

When entertaining guests, the Wrights did away with fancy china, which meant no Wedgwood or Spode; instead, they used Iroquois china that was was sold in department stores all across the county. Silver flatware, which required polishing, was replaced by practical stainless steel cutlery. Meals were served in the kitchen cafeteria-style rather than in the usual sit-down fashion of earlier days.

There's no doubt that Wright's genius shined brightest when he designed furniture with late Art Deco styling. His designs combining art and mass production were produced by the legendary firm Hey-

Skinner Auctions, Inc.

This Mid Century daybed is a version of the fainting couch from Victorian times.

Skinner Auctions, Inc.

All this 1950s Danish server needs is a laptop computer to update it to 21st century technological standards.

Treadway Toomey Galleries

It's hard to believe this credenza by Cees Braakman is almost 50 years old.

wood-Wakefield. In Wright's lifetime, his enterprises, as well as works by other designers, were usually called "Moderne," "Streamlined," or "Swedish or Danish Modern," like my Gram's blond dining suite.

When it comes to mastering Mid Century, I thought we should go to one of the very first professionals to appreciate 1950s and 1960s artifacts. For years my pal Lee Hays was a very successful antiques dealer before becoming the full-time music director of my beloved radio station, WVXU, in Cincinnati. Here is her mini autobiography concerning this fascinating area, which will help you fully understand Mid Century and how once again it became so fashionable, but this time as a semi-antique/collectible.

"When I started my career as an antique dealer in the mid-80s, I realized that items from the mid-century modern era were plentiful and reasonably priced at yard sales and auctions. Other dealers were fighting each other for Victorian walnut washstands and quilts, but there was virtually no competition for relics from the Art Deco 1950s and 1960s periods. Plus, merchandise from these time periods were pieces I had grown up with and could recognize easily. [Just like the dealer at Atlantic City said!] As my forays into mid-century modern intensified, I decided to specialize in blond Heywood-Wakefield furniture. The simple smooth lines and the fact that these pieces could mix with mid-century so well enamored itself with the buying public. I found that most of my buyers for Heywood-Wakefield furniture were aged 30-55. Many of them had grown up with the furniture and wanted to collect more to match the pieces they found in their parents' basements, bedrooms, living rooms or kitchens. Even today, the popularity of Heywood-Wakefield furniture remains strong; and you can still find pieces on television commercials and as movie set props."

Heywood-Wakefield

Heywood-Wakefield was famous for late Art Deco pieces. The firm started in 1826 in Gardner, Massachussetts, and produced a wide range of household furnishings. In 1884, a branch was established in Chicago and, by 1897, the Heywood Brothers merged with the Wakefield Rattan Company. The rest is antiques history.

Russel Wright designed a line of modern pieces for Heywood-

Skinner Auctions, Inc.

This 1960 Norwegian rosewood wall unit combines practicality and understated elegance.

Wakefield in the 1930s. However, it was not until after the Depression that the firm became a household name, much the same way Apple and Dell are for computers today. In 1937, Leo Jiranek created a modern maple line with rounded corners, wooden pulls and total streamlining. The firm continued to prosper throughout the Mid Century decades of the 1950s and 1960s, but sadly in 1979, the company—one of America's oldest—closed it doors. Then in 1994, the name Heywood-Wakefield was acquired by the South Beach Furniture Company of Miami, Florida, which then reintroduced the famous streamlined designs.

Skinner Auctions, Inc.

Heywood-Wakefield manufactured this beautifully
made walnut-stained cabinet circa 1960.

Charles and Ray Eames

Another god and goddess of Mid Century are a second husband and
wife team who designed truly timeless chairs. Charles (1907-1978)
and Bernice (Ray) Eames (1912-1988) were married in 1941, just as
America became involved in World War II. Ray was a talented modern artist, and Charles had been trained as an architect. The couple
heard that the United States Navy Department was looking for a
modern way to make splints for broken bones. The newlyweds combined skills and invented a molded plywood leg splint that helped
mend many broken bones during the war. Today, collectors display
surviving examples as sculpture!

Jackson's International Auctions

This Heywood-Wakefield three-piece set made around 1955 was perfect for the rumpus room, a 1950s term for family room.

After the war, the designer duo opened an office in Venice, California, and created three 20th century classics. In 1950, their fiberglass armchair, also known as a bucket or shell chair, became a best seller. To top that design, they created a dining chair with a plywood seat and back rest supported on steel legs. Then, in 1956, the Eameses developed a design that put them alongside Thomas Chippendale as superstars. The Herman Miller company manufactured their lounge chair with black leather seat and back supported by rosewood plywood. This model created a sensation and, in my opinion, remains the finest example of Mid Century semi-antiques.

Skinner Auctions, Inc.

Charles and Ray Eames designed this wire chair in 1951.

Hans Knoll and Florence Schust

Hans G. Knoll (1914-1955) and Florence Schust (1917-) were the "Hepburn and Tracy" of Mid Century. When the German immigrant married Florence in 1946, a romantic as well as artistic partnership was born. Their firm worked with many ultra-modern designers of the 20th century, in-

Skinner Auctions, Inc.

This icon of Mid Century was designed by Charles and Ray Eames and features black leather on molded plywood shells with walnut finish. Both were made by Herman Miller.

cluding the Art Deco deities Mies van der Rohe and Marcel Breur. After Hans tragically died in an automobile accident, Florence became president and remained so until 1960. Knoll International remains known for modern designs that personify Mid Century furniture.

Now you have a good grip on Mid Century. One more area from the not-too-distant past remains, and as you already know, Elvis is its king.

In about 1960, the legendary Marcel Breuer designed this chromium, tubular steel chair with black paint armrests and leather seat.

Skinner Auctions, Inc.

Chapter 23

Elvis: The King of Retro

Was my Aunt Panny ever right when she said, "Everybody to his/her own taste!" You are now encountering a group of semi-antiques/collectibles that is even younger than Mid Century. During my first PBS television series, *Is It Antique Yet?*, guests and I routinely made fun of beanbag chairs. Those were the days to buy old beanbag chairs, as well as the famous paintings of El on Vel. That's my polite way of saying beanbag chairs and El on Vel were about as déclassé then as Cabbage Patch dolls are today.

How things change! Today Elvis is the King of Retro, which is the chic name for semi-antiques/collectibles dating from the 1970s and

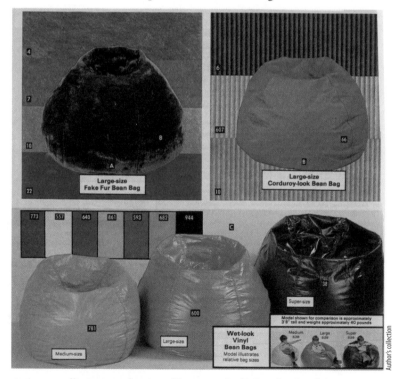

Here are several versions of the once-again-chic Retro beanbag chairs.

CLASSIC COLLECTION separates

S-t-r-e-t-c-h woven Dacron* polyester VISA* fabric "gives" a little for comfort, returns to its original shape for neatness

Order each piece in the size you need Mix and match colors for a variety of wardrobe expanding looks

ALSO IN TALL, SHORT, EXTRA TALL, BIG-TALL, BIG

Always be selective when it comes to collecting. This type of polyester, which in the 1980s was considered fabulous, is passé today.

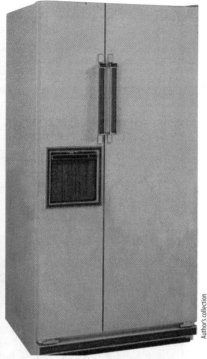

The "Golden Wheat" color of this Kenmore refrigerator was a popular Retro hue.

1980s. This heading includes beanbag chairs, lava lamps, early electronics and, of course, the King so regally captured on velvet. How grand it is that the world of antiques is ever evolving because supplies need to be constantly replenished for future collectors, which is exactly what Retro is doing.

Retro is a lot like Folk/Naïve Art antiques in the sense that there are no specific rules for what is or is not Retro. That's great news for you. Just collect anything from the 1970s or 1980s that makes you happy. Use your new-

Hard as it may be to believe, early computers fall under the Retro designation.

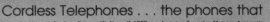

Early cordless phones are prime examples of Retro.

A hundred years from now, these corded telephones will be as popular among future collectors as Victorolas are to current collectors.

To very young collectors, 1980 microwave/convection ovens seem ancient.

Country French

Retro
reproductions of
ironstone china.

Meadowland

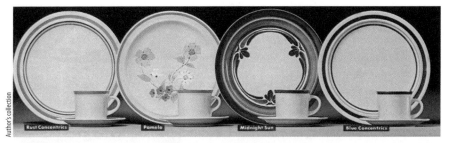

Very 1980s or Retro patterns for china.

In the 1980s, Sears offered historic patterns such as "Heritage Hall" from England.

ly acquired expertise about glass, china, silver and furniture to help guide you when collecting '70s and '80s items. The reason I suggest this is that many firms such as Wedgwood, Spode and Kirk Silver were still producing wonderful wares in those decades. Be sure to check the photos in this chapter to be completely familiar with the semi-antiques/collectibles that have made El on Vel the King!

The best news of all is that Retro is still mighty affordable compared to older antiques such as Queen Anne or 1900s oak furniture. So now is the perfect time to stock up while Retro goodies are still plentiful and available at flea markets and garage sales. Rest assured that in another 10 years Retro items will acquire fancy price tags in swanky antiques shops and malls.

Author's collection

Sears described these chairs as having a "fruitwood finish," a trendy term in Mid Century and Retro days that meant a medium-brown tone.

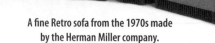

A fine Retro sofa from the 1970s made by the Herman Miller company.

Treadway Toomey Galleries

THE SEATING

ROCKERS mean
relaxing comfort
and classic styling,
whether the decor is
colonial, traditional
or contemporary

(A) Homestead Boston Rocker
CONSTRUCTION: Selected hardwoods.
Turnings on legs and posts. High spindle
back. Gold-color silk-screened headrail decoration on maple and pine finish rockers. No
decoration on white finish rocker. All finishes
have a clear lacquer coating for added protection. Measures 24x29x37 in. high; seat
21x18 in. deep. More matching Homestead
furnishings sold on pages 1214-15, 1276-77.
ORDERING INFORMATION: Assembled. See
"N" note, page 580.
Shipping weight 21 pounds.
1 A 17517N—*Maple finish* $49.99
1 A 17512N—*Pine finish* 49.99
1 A 17506N—*White finish* 49.99

(B) Contemporary-style Rocker
CONSTRUCTION: Solid beechwood. Clear
lacquer finish. Spindle back. Measures
22x19x42 inches high; seat 22x19 in. deep.
ORDERING INFORMATION: Assembled. See
"N" note on page 580.
1 A 17157N—Shpg. wt. 22 lbs. . . . $159.99

(C) Deluxe Bentwood Rocker
CONSTRUCTION: Genuine steambent solid
beechwood frame and legs. Seat and back
made of handwoven natural cane. Walnut or
natural finish with clear lacquer coating for
added protection. Measures 19x41x40½
inches high; seat 18x21½ inches deep.
ORDERING INFORMATION: Unassembled.
See "N" suffix note on page 580.
Shipping weight 20 pounds.
1 A 17561N—*Walnut* $119.99
1 A 17562N—*Natural* 119.99

(D) Early-American-style rocker
CONSTRUCTION: Solid hardwood. Turned
posts. Saddle-shaped seat and slat back. Finish has clear lacquer coating for added protection. Measures 21½x18x39½ inches high;
seat measures 21x18 inches deep.
ORDERING INFORMATION: Assembled. See
"N" note, page 580. Shpg. wt. 22 lbs.
1 A 17163N—Maple finish $79.99
1 A 17164N—Pine finish 79.99

**(E) Firecrest Early-American
Catkin Rocker**
CONSTRUCTION: Solid hardwood. Turned
posts. Saddle-shaped seat and slat back. Pine
finish with clear lacquer coating for added
protection. Measures 33x25½x41 inches
high; seat 18x21½ inches deep.
ORDERING INFORMATION: Assembled. See
"N" suffix note, page 580.
1 A 17153N—Shpg. wt. 34 lbs. . . . $119.99

(F) Open-Hearth Rocker
CONSTR: Solid beechwood. Husky turned
posts. Saddle-shaped seat and slat back. Pine
finish with silk-screened crown decoration
and hand-painted gold-color striping; clear
lacquer coated. Measures 25¾x31x45¼ in.
high; seat 18½x22½ in. deep.
Assembled. See "N" suffix note on page 580.
1 A 17151N—Shpg. wt. 45 lbs. . . . $159.99

(G) Nostalgia Rocker
CONSTRUCTION: Solid beechwood. Decorative embossed crown. Turned posts. Spindle
back. Antique oak finish with clear lacquer
coating. Measures 18½x23x42½ inches high;
seat 18x18½ inches deep.
ORDERING INFORMATION: Assembled. See
"N" suffix note on page 580.
1 A 17142N—Shpg. wt. 27 lbs. . . . $159.99

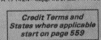
*Credit Terms and
States where applicable
start on page 559*

1220 | Sears | ALL

Author's collection

Even rocking chairs like these 1982 models got the Retro treatment.

SECTION THREE

Antiques Classics

Chapter 24

China: Bottoms Up for Identification and Dating

In days gone by, referring to dining paraphernalia as "china" indicated refinement, while the term "dishes" (the more correct term from an academic point of view), was considered a trite gauche. Gram never took her grandson to the "dish" department at the great Chicago emporium Marshall Field's. We went instead to the "china" floor, as she always called it. All this jargon may seem somewhat confusing, but shortly the various terminology concerning what we serve our burgers or crab cakes on will become as plain as the white background on an antique soup tureen.

Ceramics

To become skilled with these special antiques, let's go back to classical times. Wise Greeks correctly described objects made from clay (the main ingredient for both china and dishes) as "ceramics." So if you want to be totally accurate in your antiques jargon, use the word "ceramics." Incidentally, the term "dishes" is a general term that refers to the various classifications of ceramics included in this chapter.

Capo de Monte of Naples is Italy's most famous ceramic maker.

Jackson's International Auctions

Clay, the main ingredient for any ceramic, is primarily aluminum silicate, a malleable soil coming from crumbling rocks. What determines the final category of ceramic is the type of clay from which it is made and the temperature and the length of time at which the mixture is fired.

Although many categories of ceramics exist, all have the same crucial ingredient and have been made in the same manner. Wet clay is kneaded to remove air bubbles, and shaping may be accomplished by either of two methods. The first involves throwing clay on a potter's wheel. Pumping a foot pedal connected to an axle creates a circular motion for a flat disc that allows the skilled potter's hand to form various vessels.

In the second method, clay is liquefied by adding water and poured into a mold to dry. The object is in the "cheese" state when it is removed from the mold and fired in a kiln until hard. The resulting product is known as "biscuit" or "bisque." Decorations are hand painted or decals applied using a process called "transfer" (to be explained shortly). Glazing, the final stage, produces a glass-like coating that protects decorations. A final firing in the kiln renders the piece totally waterproof.

Porcelain

The "china" versus "dishes" debate dates long before Gram—and, in fact, a few centuries before the discovery of the New World. Let's start with porcelain to learn how this squabble began.

Loomism

To easily identify porcelain, hold it up to the light to see its translucency. The object should be quite hard and lightweight.

Because the very white clay called kaolin remains white after firing, it is used for porcelain. Deposits of kaolin were first discovered in China, where porcelain was developed. Later, when the precious ingredient was found in Germany, England, and the United States, Westerners were also able to produce this magical ceramic.

Marco Polo's legendary grand tour of China triggered the Western frenzy for porcelain. Polo (1254-1324) was a very early European visitor to China, and upon returning to his native Venice, he introduced numerous Chinese novelties such as toilet tissue and gunpowder.

Marco Polo's souvenirs truly revealed the backward state of Europe in the late 1200s compared to China. This was particularly evident with European ceramics, which were thick, clunky and artistically

Mention German antiques and most of us immediately think of steins.

Forsythes' Auctions

unappealling. To Europeans, the Chinese sensation was a high-tech wonder, much the same way early television was at the 1939 Worlds Fair. This beautiful, thin, scratch-resistant ceramic marked the debut of an antiques superstar. Unfortunately, right from its dazzling European unveiling, the technically correct name "porcelain" was rarely used. The phenomenon was christened "china" in honor of its homeland. The name has endured to the present, and remarkably, all sorts of ceramics have been called "china."

The proper term, "porcelain," or what Europeans called "the Chinese wonder," originated in France and meant "Venus shell." A seashell and a porcelain teacup exhibit the same degree of translucency when held up to bright sunlight. Porcelain, like shell, has a lightweight body very different from heavier opaque European ceramics that were standard before the arrival of this oriental marvel.

Porcelain was made in China as early as 960 A.D. A totally white version was labeled "blanc-de-Chine," meaning "white from China." Several color combinations were successful, yet one extraordinary duo became the "Jeanette MacDonald and Nelson Eddy" of Chinese porcelain (and later, of European versions, too). Just as those 1930s songbirds are synonymous with Hollywood musicals, the same is true of Chinese blue and white. Pieces in this charismatic twosome produced in the Chinese cities of Nanking and Canton became known as "Chinese Export." Examples of these wares that belonged to the Washington family await your ogling at Mount Vernon.

European Porcelain

GERMAN PORCELAIN

Germans at Meissen in the Saxony region began producing porcelain after kaolin was discovered there in 1709. After finding this vital material, artisans learned that a very high temperature was crucial. When it comes to fine German porcelain, the terms "Meissen" and "Dresden" are interchangeable. Both refer to where the celebrated porcelain was produced. "Meissen" refers to the town, while "Dresden" is the name of the district. Figurines and candlesticks dating from the 1700s were decorated with Rococo motifs such as flowers or cherubs. In true Gilded Age spirit, heavy gilt abounded on most examples from the mid-1800s.

This highly esteemed German porcelain is usually marked with crossed swords. Be careful, though, because this German iconic blue label has often been faked. Buy from reputable retailers and get accurate descriptions on your receipts guaranteeing authenticity.

Jackson's International Auctions

Hutschenreuther of Germany made this set in the "Carolin Magnus" pattern in the early 20th century.

BRITISH PORCELAIN

After kaolin was found in Cornwall in 1770, the English began fashioning porcelain. The savvy Brits perfected porcelain and other ceramics under the free enterprise system. Unlike royal counterparts on the Continent, the George Hanovers never granted government funds to British potteries. By 1842, 17 British porcelain factories had been established, including Spode, Coalport, Wedgwood, and Worcester. How reassuring in these days of business buyouts that such distinguished firms are still booming and making future antiques.

Royal Worcester of England is one of the most beloved china makers of all time.

Around 1800, the English improved porcelain by adding ground bone ash from farm animals to wet kaolin clay. But following tradition, the more precise term "bone porcelain" was never chosen. Consequently, the technically incorrect, but ever-so-swanky-sounding term "bone china" was adopted. This updated porcelain was even more light-

Franciscan Pottery, originally made in California, and now part of Wedgwood, was famous for its "Apple" pattern.

Copeland-Spode's famous "Indian Tree" pattern, based on an Oriental motif, has become classic.

weight, translucent,and stronger than standard porcelain. Bone china is always the mark of quality, and like Gram said, it doesn't chip as easily as its boneless cousins.

FRENCH PORCELAIN

In 1673, the French started porcelain production in Rouen, the city where the English (during one of the numerous skirmishes with the French) executed Joan of Arc. A factory in Sevres, near Paris, has been creating porcelain masterpieces since 1756. Louis XV granted the enterprise royal funds during its early years. The monarch's generosity came about thanks to his mistress, Madame de Pompadour, who had amassed about 2,500 pieces of Sevres.

Queen Marie Antoinette was also a big fan; her Sevres services were often adorned with her regal monogram "M.A." Ornate examples from the 1700s duplicated Rococo styles and, during the mid-1800s, Sevres replicated the lavishness of Rococo Revival. By the late 1800s, huge cobalt-blue urns festooned with gilt and floral motifs decorated swanky mansions on Nob Hill, Fifth Avenue, Peachtree Street and Lake Shore Drive.

As the mid-1800s arrived, Americans became enraptured with another French ceramic. This is the most famous of all French porcelains and was named after Limoges, a city in southern France. Its

This porcelain punch bowl was made in Limoges, France, and then hand decorated in the United States by John Anton Coufall for Pickard China, a famous Yankee firm.

Jackson's International Auctions

nearby kaolin deposits made the town a prime location for porcelain manufacturers. Many factories existed, but one in particular comes to the head of the Limoges class. The most illustrious name remains "Haviland," founded by David Haviland. This ex-Yankee started his company in Limoges during the 1840s when he began exporting massive sets to the United States.

Incidentally, the famous Hollywood actress Olivia de Havilland (yes, with two l's), who played Melanie in *Gone With the Wind*, is purportedly a relative of the firm's founder. By 1900, Limoges was as synonymous with French china as Detroit would become to American automobiles.

In the 1890s, Sears sold Limoges floral motif dinner sets through its catalogues. The arrays included every imaginable piece needed to serve 12 for a mere $39.45. Other fine makers included Elite, T.V. Brand and Arnfeldt. Miraculously, some of these venerated firms are still creating future antiques.

Here is a delightful tidbit about Limoges and an incomparable artist. Limoges was also the hometown of Pierre Renoir (1841-1919), who at 14 apprenticed as a china decorator. His training bode well and helped create such masterpieces as "On the Terrace," which thrills visitors at the Art Institute of Chicago.

Earthenware

The ceramics in use before the Chinese sensation seduced Europeans are remarkable antiques in their own right. The few Europeans who could even afford dishes usually had a very old type of ceramic. Pottery or earthenware was made from nonwhite (usually reddish) clay fired at a lower temperature than needed for porcelain. Glazing was especially crucial for this thick, opaque and porous ceramic to protect decorations and render them waterproof.

IRONSTONE

Ironstone, a famous earthenware, was invented by Miles Mason in 1797. Since it was heavy, durable and economical, ironstone became the Corningware of the 1800s. This product from Staffordshire generally graced cottages, bungalows and farmhouses rather than the grand dining rooms of palatial residences.

The Mason firm became so successful that by 1813 Miles' son

Charles finally took out a patent. The mark read: "Mason's Patent Ironstone China." This clever family of potters realized the clout of using the word "china." Mason's Ironstone, a beloved antique firm, is part of the present Wedgwood Group. Current products will one day become treasured antiques. A client told me that her antique ironstone is even microwaveable, which is quite a testimony to its practicality. Other renowned makers included Johnson Brothers, Meakin, Adams and Alcock. These firms used various names for their versions such as "stoneware," "stone china" and "Pearlware," all of which are interchangeable with "ironstone."

MAJOLICA

Majolica is a trendy ceramic constantly touted in magazines and on television. This name describes thick earthenware with a heavy glaze over brightly colored raised designs. The pottery originated on the island of Majolica off the coast of Spain. In the 1300s and into the 1400s, the Italians were creating their own renditions. By the late 1800s, colorful motifs depicting cabbages, fruits, ferns and asparagus were being created in France, Germany and England. A number of manufacturers clearly marked their wares, which helps dating. They include Wedgwood, Minton, and George Jones of Great Britain. American firms were George Morley and Griffen, Smith, and Hill.

In the late 1800s, Wedgwood was known for its Majolica line.

Even the Germans made Majolica, such as these radiantly hued plates dating from the late 1800s.

Jackson's International Auctions

Transfer Decoration

While Europeans were making various types of ceramics, many other aspects of the business were undergoing changes. The technological advances of the Industrial Revolution transformed the ceramic business, especially in England.

TRANSFER DESIGN

Decorating china before 1750 involved labor-intensive hand painting. The Industrial Revolution quickly modernized the process. In Liverpool, England, the partners Sadler and Green invented modern transfer printing—a process similar to applying decals—to decorate china. A scene was first engraved on a copper sheet and then inked and printed on very thin paper. The paper was then moistened and carefully placed on the unglazed ceramic before the ink dried. As the paper dissolved, the inked design, like a decal, was transferred to the piece.

Royal Copenhagen of Denmark is usually associated with blue and white designs, but this colorful set is appropriately known as "Flora."

Transfer printing, a major advancement of the Industrial Revolution, accelerated production, which in turn increased quantities and reduced prices. Thanks to their ingenuity, the Brits became to ceramics what the Japanese would become to electronics. Transfer printing made the Staffordshire region, (about two-and-a-half hours north of London), a world-famous center for reasonably priced, yet quality ceramics.

FLOW BLUE

In the early days before transfer printing was perfected, a unique design inadvertently developed. Like its name suggests, Flow Blue is earthenware with smeared blue designs on a white background. As the design transferred, the ink flowed or smudged, creating a charming so-called flaw that today is fervently collected. Staffordshire potteries in the 1820s, including Adams, Wedgwood, Alcock, and Ridgway, created neoclassical motifs depicting large urns laden with huge bouquets of flowers. By the 1860s, flowers or cherubs in the Rococo Revival taste were popular themes.

STAFFORDSHIRE BLUE AND WHITE

Transfer printing experimented with numerous colors, but as with Chinese porcelain, blue and white proved the most appealing. By the

Skinner Auctions, Inc.)

An English firm made this dinner service in the mid-1800s. The "Ancient Ruins" transfer pattern is a prime example of Flow Blue.

Examples of English transfer from the early 1800s, known as "Staffordshire," after the area of its origin.

early 1800s, Staffordshire makers were finally able to duplicate that sparkling duo recalling white clouds on a sunny blue sky. Today, antique "Staffordshire" with blue and white designs continues to dazzle collectors.

Woods Ware, made in the Staffordshire region of England is a beloved china maker, especially for aficionados of blue and white.

Jackson's International Auctions

Early Auction Company

Blue and white Canton porcelain from China, like these pieces from the 1800s, has enjoyed enduring popularity among collectors.

Skinner Auctions, Inc.

What a superb display of Oriental ceramics! The blue and white are examples
of Canton, while the orange, green and pink pieces are Rose Medallion.

British china makers recognizing a money-making opportunity
cranked out souvenirs immortalizing the grand farewell tour of an
American Revolutionary War hero. In 1826, General Washington's
French assistant during the American Revolution returned to America—his "second country"—for one final hurrah. The aged Marquis de
Lafayette was fêted all across the young republic. One stellar soirée
was hosted at Montpelier, the Virginia plantation home of President
James Madison and First Lady Dolley.

How amusing that a former enemy of Great Britain was glorified
on English Staffordshire china. "Business is business," thought the
practical Brits, thus reflecting another antique example of global economics.

DELFT

Delft is another blue and white ceramic that is an enduring star in the
world of antiques. In the late 1600s, the Dutch in the city of Delft were
the first Europeans to successfully duplicate the unique Chinese blue
and white. "Delft" pieces usually had designs of windmills and other
themes associated with the Netherlands. Look for "Delft," "Holland"
or "made in Holland" to help you identify genuine Delft.

These colorful vases, dating from the late 1800s and early 1900s, are fine examples of Nippon.

WILLOW PATTERN

British Josiah Spode originated the oriental-inspired Willow design around 1810 to cash in on the popularity of blue-and-white Chinese porcelain. In antiquese, this motif is called "Chinoiserie," meaning "Chinese-looking." The English version of Canton includes a willow tree, two pagodas, two birds and three people crossing a bridge. This Western creation proved to be the most popular china pattern of all time—so much so that the Brits, Yanks and even the Japanese produced Willow versions. Although the motif came in a myriad of colors, blue and white has remained first choice among collectors.

Japanese Ceramics

Since the late 1800s, Japan has been a tough competitor with the Brits, Europeans and Yankees in the china department. Japanese ceramics were less expensive, yet equal in quality to most Western products. In the early 1900s, Sears and Ward's sold Japanese goods in its catalogues. A particular bestseller was vases with heavy gilt decoration encasing a hand-painted landscape. After 1891, these beauties were usually marked "Nippon," which is the Japanese word for "Japan."

Bottoms Up for Dating

Just think "bottoms up" to tell the age of ceramics. Many pieces are unmarked with nothing to indicate age. Perhaps this means that it dates before 1891, or the modern paper label has been removed. As I have said before, global economies and concerns over balance of trade are as old as the antiques we collect. The McKinley Tariff Act of 1891 protected American industries by ruling that foreign items entering the United States must be marked with the country of origin.

Dating English pieces makes learning about ceramics a lot easier. Once you master this group, you're ready to tackle other countries. Before 1891, a Willow plate made by Doulton in Staffordshire only had the Doulton logo. After 1891, "England" was included, which dates the plate between 1891 and World War I. Labels with "Made in" added to "England" suggest a post-1918 date. This can help you date china from all over the world, whether Italian, German or Chinese.

One unique exception concerns Japan. In compliance with the McKinley Tariff Act, Japanese makers marked pieces "Nippon," which, as I pointed out earlier, is the Japanese word for "Japan." "Nippon" indicates production between 1891 and 1921. By 1921, the American government had ordered the word "Japan" to be used rather than "Nippon." In time, "Made in" was also added. Whether labeled "Nippon" or "Japan," this china remains a best-selling antique.

OCCUPIED JAPAN

Here is a Japanese mark that's foolproof for dating. Ceramics made at the end of World War II during the American occupation were marked "Made in Occupied Japan." When you find this mark, you know your semi-antique dates from 1945 to 1952.

Following are more secrets for dating china that I have learned through the years.

Twentieth-century china requires less knowledge to pinpoint dates than you might think. The more information on china the younger it is. Keep this principle in mind, and you'll quickly become proficient at dating pieces. A plate that says "acid resisting colors" indicates the Depression era. "Dishwasher safe" designates the *I Love Lucy* decade; and obviously, "microwavable" means the mid-1970s to the present.

Loomism

The more information on china, the younger it is.

The mark on a certain brand-new plate reads: "Since 1883 Johnson Brothers has been making fine tableware for over 100 years, establishing a proud reputation for craftsmanship and quality of designs. Old British Castles, copyright Johnson Brothers 1929, made in England." Since that label is practically an encyclopedia of information, you can see that my Loomism is right on target. Here's more good news: this Loomism works just as well for other antiques like furniture and silver. Once in a while, an exception pops up, but this guide will help you many, many times. So keep in mind, the more information on an item, the newer it is.

More Tricks for Dating

Here are some other methods I have developed for determining age. The transfer design on the Johnson Brothers "British Castles" plate that I just mentioned is as precise as an etching on paper. Decorations on older pieces such as 1930s "Vista" by Mason's are not nearly as clear-cut as younger versions. An even older transfer plate marked only by its maker, "Wedgwood," or "Ridgway's," (without country), indicates pre-1891 production. Besides that clue to late 1800s production, another is that the designs on Wedgwood and Ridgway pieces have a "smudgy" look compared to the more precise 20th century examples.

When I toured the incredible Wedgwood Museum in Stoke-on-Trent, England, I learned how furniture styles often influenced ceramics. That is your antiques coach's rationale for emphasizing furniture designs so much for your introduction to antiques. Once you have furniture styles (the easiest and most fun to learn) glued in your mental scrapbook, learning other antiques will be a breeze. So when you spot a floral design on a teapot that reminds you of Rococo Revival furniture, you can accurately determine that the teapot dates from the 1850s or 1860s.

Here is the only reference book ever needed to date British china. Go to the art and music department of your public library and scan *The Encyclopedia for British Pottery and Porcelain Marks* by Geoffrey A. Godden (Crown Publishers). Through the years I have worn out my copy.

This reference is very enlightening. Some years ago, I checked my Gram's most prized heirloom, her good china. The service belonged to her beloved older sister, our great Aunt Nana, and was decorated with Oriental trees and flowers and marked "Soho Pottery Cobridge, England." The precisely printed pattern name indicated a 20th century production. An older label would have had more flourishes in the true Rococo Revival spirit of the mid-1800s. "England" was also included, which helped date Aunt Nana's china from 1906 to about World War I.

When it comes to dating china from countries other than Great Britain, there is considerably less organization, so just follow "the country of origin" and "made in" generalization for dating, and you'll be on target.

Have you ever heard someone state with an air of authority a remark similar to this: "It belonged to Bill's great-grandmother who died in 1935 at the age of 90. So it has to be over 100 years old." Unfortunately, the person could have made that estimate based on the inaccurate assumption that the tea service dates from her birth in 1845. Of course, it could very well have been a wedding present in 1865, or a gift for a 50th wedding anniversary in 1915, or grandma could have bought it herself in 1934. Unlike movie stars, whose birthdates are routinely rolled forward, the age of family antiques are commonly (though usually unintentionally) exaggerated in the opposite direction.

Loomism

Family members tend to exaggerate the age of heirlooms.

Now that the various terminologies for ceramics are as plain as the white background of antique tureens, let's continue using the delightful antique misnomer "china." Since past gentility is a treasure to relish, how absolutely right our ancestors were to prefer "china" over the more correct word "dishes" for their porcelain, earthenware and other ceramics.

Chapter 25

Silver:
A Sterling Antique

Just as there are china aficionados and furniture enthusiasts, a huge group of collectors crave antique silver. If you have a hankering for dining with a flair, then this splendid antique may just be your tonic.

The word "silver" is derived from the Greek word "argyos," meaning "bright and shiny." Crafting silver goes as far back in history as making glass, furniture or pottery.

Silver articles fall under two classifications: hollowware and flatware. Hollowware includes bowls, tankards, teapots and religious items such as chalices, beakers and spice boxes. Flatware encompasses knives, forks, spoons and other utensils.

Jackson's International Auctions

Victorians were fond of displaying silver plate baskets or centerpieces such as this sensational example made by Meriden Silver in the 1880s.

Pure silver is soft and must be strengthened with copper to make it suitable for table use. Artisans have added copper to melted silver for centuries, but in about 1300, during the reign of Edward I, English silversmiths created the sterling standard to regulate the quantity of copper. Sterling silver is an alloy of 925 parts silver to 75 parts copper. Although sterling is not pure silver, this formula is as close to 100 percent as is practical.

The word "sterling" may have evolved from "Easterling," the family name of a group of German silversmiths working in England during the Middle Ages. Another theory credits the name to "starling," or little star, an early mark for English silver.

British Hallmarks

The very structured British hallmark system deserves praise. This system for labeling silver objects reveals age, city of origin, the silversmith and sometimes even more. Practice locating such hallmarks on a spoon, which are usually on the underside of the midsection of the handle or under the bowl. On teapots or other hollowware, these marks may be somewhat less obvious. Take your time looking on rims of bowls and teapots and on the underside of trays.

To be sterling, an English piece must be emblazoned with a crouching lion, called "le Lion Rampant," in a rectangular area. This identification, conceived in London around 1554, I have nicknamed "Leo the Lion." To determine if a piece is English sterling, look for "Leo."

"Leo the Lion" is the only hallmark that warrants memorization because there are many fine books in the art and music department of your public library that can help decode other marks.

Victorians had special dining accoutrements, such as this vintage 1875 silver plate pickle castor. This model by Meriden even had a fork and tongs on each side.

Remaining hallmarks are usually jumbled without any order. Since these designations have many variations, don't try to memorize them; rather, keep those reference books handy. After "Leo," the next most important mark identifies the origin of an object. Verifying location is the key to deciphering the remaining marks because each city has its own symbol. The blazon of a leopard's head seems ironically jovial for majestic London. Others include an anchor for Birmingham, a crown for Sheffield, a harp for Dublin, and several more, which are listed in reference books.

The next hallmark reveals age. The highly regulated English devised this handy system around 1438. Look for one letter in a box, which is the code for the year the object was made. Match the letters under the city of origin to determine the year.

In 1784, the profile of the ruling monarch

How clever the Victorians were! This cranberry glass bowl with silver plate lid, circa 1880, held sugar, while side notches were for displaying spoons. This novelty is sometimes called a spooner.

This silver plate water server by Wilcox Silver Company, circa 1875, was an early example of a thermos. Its lining helped keep drinking water chilled while adding panache to the sideboard.

The Pairpoint Silver firm created this plated castor set around 1880. It held vinegar, oil, salt, and pepper in glass castors.

when an item was crafted became an additional hallmark. Such royal data makes identifying more recent silver even easier. The silhouette of George III dates an item from his reign. The outline of a svelte Queen Victoria reveals an 1840s origin, while a mature, more rotund depiction indicates her later years. And, of course, her successors, such as Edward VI, have their profiles featured as well.

The maker's monogram is another important hallmark. For example, on pieces easily identified as made in London (thanks to the leopard's head), you may find the intials "H.B." The London section of reference books attributes that monogram to Hester Bateman. (More about this incomparable silver artisan is in an upcoming chapter.)

One more trick that will help you distinguish sterling from silverplated pieces is that sterling pieces feel lightweight and seem almost bendable. Plated pieces, on the other hand, feel heavier and more rigid. This handy rule of thumb will help you distinguish sterling from plated pieces.

Furniture Know-How

What if a silver antique is flirting with you in an antiques mall, and no references are quickly accessible? Since silver designs followed furniture trends, familiarity with antique furniture helps to accurately guesstimate age. For example, let's say you spot a pepper castor (shaker) with feet resembling cabriole legs. Our furniture know-how reveals that those trifid feet (the fancy silver term) date the castor from the Queen Anne period of the mid-1700s. A superornate teapot covered with spooky designs so typical of a Renaissance Revival sideboard indicates an 1880s vintage.

Continental Silver

Mastering European silver—whether German, French or Italian—is beyond the scope of *Antiques 101* for several reasons. First, Continentals rarely marked wares as clearly or with such orderliness as the Brits. Second, Europeans commonly used slightly different silver/copper blends: 800 parts silver/200 parts copper, 825 parts silver/175 parts copper, and 835 parts silver/165 parts copper. If marked at all, pieces were discreetly and minutely labeled .800, .825, or .835. Although European silver has more copper than British, keep in mind that Continental silver still has the featherweight feel so common to British sterling. Such "hands-on" awareness will facilitate your silver sleuthing.

If European silver should ever wink at you before antiques graduate school, it should present no dilemma for you. Your antique furniture knowledge will guide you to make correct guesstimates, even about Continental silver. In the meantime, master British and Yankee silver to get in shape for tackling Continental pieces if that should become your antique silver cup of tea.

Coin Silver

Yankee silversmiths didn't follow the British standard for sterling until the mid-1800s. Rather, they favored the coin gauge, which used 900 parts silver and 100 parts copper. While pieces were not usually identified as "coin," the silversmith's name was typically noted on the underside. Several good references listing American makers can be found at the library.

During Colonial times, New England prospered as a silver center. Around 1659, Hull and Sanderson were early, successful American silversmiths, but another was an incredible silversmith and a valiant messenger.

Paul Revere: An American Superstar

The superstar of American silver remains Paul Revere II (1735-1818) of Boston. This descendant of French Protestants created astounding neoclassical silver, which in furniture terms we know as Hepplewhite, Sheraton, or "Heppleton." During the American Revolution, the Bostonian's patriotism only enhanced his reputation, even though his business, by necessity, suffered neglect. Henry Wasdsworth Long-fellow's poem "The Midnight Ride of Paul Revere," cemented his legendary status as zealous patriot, while increasing his stature as silversmith.

After Longfellow's poetic commemoration, Revere achieved superstar status when hollowware based on his neoclassical style became traditional wedding presents. For over a century, handsomely understated silver "Revere" bowls and pitchers have been received by millions of appreciative brides.

Just before the Civil War, American silver makers switched to the British standard for sterling silver. During this period of transition from coin to sterling, "925/1000" was engraved on the underside of silver pieces. By the 1870s and 1880s, the word "sterling" had replaced the numerical mark and indicated post-Civil War production.

Production Methods

Before modern production, whether in England or America or on the Continent, sliversmiths made hollowware by rolling or hammering silver into thin sheets, then beating the sheets on an anvil with a mallet to shape them into teapots, bowls or other pieces. Decoration was added by chasing or piercing. Chasing was akin to engraving the surface. Piercing involved creating a series of holes in the upper sides of bowls, producing a basket-like appearance. This reticulated motif had originated centuries earlier in Chinese porcelain. Fine flatware—or cutlery as the Brits say—was made by pouring melted sterling into molds to form knives, forks and other pieces.

Repoussé

The most stunning decoration for silver hollowware or flatware was justly granted a beguiling French name. Although a variation of this pattern had been around for years, Samuel Kirk (1793-1872) of Baltimore recognized the panache of stylish French and christened his version "Repoussé." His magnificent name is another exception to my Loomism about avoiding French terms. The English translation of Repoussé is "pushed out." While the English phrase makes the meaning clearer, it most definitely lacks the grace and beauty of the French ver-

Jackson's International Auctions

The most adored American silver pattern for flatware
is the magical "Repoussé" first created by Samuel Kirk.

sion. At auctions today antique "Repoussé" fetches prices far higher than most other silver patterns.

Crafting "Repoussé" takes a great deal of skill because the nearly three-dimensional decoration (or "bas relief" in fancy terms) is crafted by hammering the underside of thin silver pieces. Such a design created from underneath is literally "pushed out" or "Repoussé," as Mr. Kirk more charmingly stated. Mr. Revere may remain the most famous American silversmith, but his later colleague, Samuel Kirk, made "Repoussé" the most renowned pattern for American silver.

Silver Plate

As I said earlier, sterling sliver and coin silver pieces are noticeably lighter than silver plate. Also, both sterling and coin have a flexible feeling compared to extra-rigid silver plate. A silver or coin spoon bends easily, while plated remains far more unyielding because of the underlying base metal.

Sheffield

By the mid-1700s, the British had devised a method for making silver plated copper. In 1742, Thomas Boulsover of Sheffield, England, invented the process of encasing copper in silver. By the 1790s, Sheffield dominated English silver plate, just as Staffordshire ruled as the center of English china.

Sheffield has become a generic term referring to the 1700s hand plating technique originated in that city. The procedure resembled making a cheese sandwich, with the silver sheets being the bread, and the copper center the cheese. Two thin silver sheets were placed over a thick piece of copper. By hammering the metal "sandwich" with a mallet on an anvil, a teapot, tray or other hollowware item was formed. Although less expensive than sterling, labor-intensive Sheffield still remained out of reach of most households.

Sheffield plate was rarely marked, but if you should find a hallmark, refer once again to the reference books in the art and music department of your library. Because of the copper center, Sheffield plate is much heftier and stiffer than sterling or coin hollowware. Through years of use, the outer silver on Sheffield frequently wore away, revealing the inner copper. Time has the same effect on furniture, as costly veneered mahogany on drawer fronts flakes off, exposing less choice pine. These examples of patina, or "the kiss of time," make our antiques look venerable in a lovely way.

Silver and the Industrial Revolution

As machines were producing many household goods at far more affordable prices than ever before, manufacturers were looking to technology to achieve the same results with silver and silver plate. Machinery did manage to produce sterling silver articles, but science was about to unlock the key to revolutionize the production of silver plate.

Around 1840, the Elkington Brothers of Birmingham, England, in true Industrial Revolution spirit, applied for a patent for a novel method of creating silver plate. Modern electroplating modernized the plating business.

In the new process, "white" metal (actually silver colored) hollowware was quickly molded rather than hand shaped. Then the item was dipped in a bath containing an electrolytic solution. When an electric current passed through the solution, silver bonded evenly to the surface. The amount of silver coating depended upon the length of the immersion.

Like other goods produced during the Industrial Revolution, faster manufacturing reduced labor costs and increased inventories. Electroplating dropped prices far below what Sheffield could possibly offer. Sadly, that put most Sheffield makers out of business, and pewter makers met the same fate, which is detailed in the next chapter.

In 1847, the Roger Brothers in the United States began using the electroplating process for making silver plate hollowware and flatware. Rumors still persist that these fellows swiped the technology from the Elkington firm.

English and American plate don't have the "Leo the Lion" mark, the word "Sterling," or the numerals "925/1000." Ironically, the word "Sheffield" on plate indicates electroplating that's not the genuine handmade Sheffield. British pieces were sometimes marked "E.P.N.S.," standing for Electroplate on Nickel Silver. Nickel silver plate was the white metal that was encased in silver. American pieces were usually labeled with the manufacturer's name. Gorham, Wallace, and Reed & Barton are three prominent Yankee firms. Sometimes you'll find the words "triple dipped" or three stars marked on a piece, indicating a

Such a handsome sterling silver tea service must have been the pride and joy of a Flapper bride. Trays including this one were usually silver plate, not of chintziness, but of necessity. Stronger silver plate was needed for support when every silver piece was full.

Garth's Auctions, Inc.

Forsythes' Auctions

Notice the geometrical Art Deco design of this sterling silver tea-and-coffee service dating from the late 1920s or 1930s. The tray, as you now know, is silver plate.

triple coat of silver, truly a quality touch.

My Loomism stating that "the more information on ceramics, the newer it is" also applies to silver. The more facts detailed on a mark, such as dimensions, pattern name, or other tidbits, the newer the silver or plate piece is.

As you know so well, mass production dramatically increased quantities and reduced prices, which was especially fortuitous timing. As the middle and upper class swelled during Queen Victoria's reign, so did their craving for silver. During her rule, practically everything imaginable, whether in sterling for the wealthy, or plate for the newly flourishing middle class, was eagerly sought.

Studying antiques reveals how nothing really changes—only the players. These days, athletic equipment is as multifaceted as old-time dining accoutrements. Each sport, it seems, demands special shoes and clothing. During La Belle Époque, as the French call the 1890s and early 1900s, the same held true for flatware.

Decorum required a myriad of cutlery for proper dining. Here is a sampling of just the spoons deemed so essential for stylish dinners: a small spoon for after-dinner coffee, a pointed one for melons, a really tiny rendition for salt cellars, a small rounded version for cream soups, a smaller rounded model if bouillon were served, a big spoon with an oval bowl for desserts, and if that weren't enough, a half-spoon and half-fork combination known as an ice cream fork, for cake served with ice cream.

Punch Bowls

Here's a final sparkling anecdote about a special silver antique to polish off your introduction to antique silver. By World War I, the punch bowl, or "Monteith" bowl, had achieved a rather high social standing and had become a fashionable wedding present rivaling Revere bowls and pitchers. But a shady tale of the bowl's origin has existed for centuries. According to legend, in the 1600s a Scottish bon vivant named Monteith was the first to give real punch to punch by adding booze. Eventually, silver bowls with notches in the rim for holding stemmed glasses became known as "Monteith" bowls in tribute to the creative trailblazer who really knew how to add zip to gatherings. Who knows if the account is really true, but, nevertheless, the story helps us remember Monteith bowls.

Antique Sheffield plate can be very expensive, while old electroplate offers real bargains because it does not have a high resale value. In simple terms, that means there are deals everywhere. A plated tea service usually costs 75 percent less than a sterling set. And best of all, sterling and plate tarnish at the same rate, so no one but you (and your antiques coach) will know whether it is sterling or plate.

Let's now look at a cousin of silver that once was for working folk, but has recently become quite an upscale antique.

Chapter 26

Pewter: Silver's Humble (Yet Trendy) Cousin

In both Great Britain and the United States, the premier era for furnishings in Chippendale, Hepplewhite, Sheraton and Empire styles also marked the peak years for pewter. During that time, household accessories crafted from pewter were middle-of-the-road versions of costlier silver pieces.

Pewter is a manmade alloy, or mixture of metals, created to resemble silver. Its main ingredient is tin with small amounts of lead, copper, antimony and, for durability, bismuth. Pewter is heavier and duller looking than silver, which makes it easy to distinguish from its aristocratic cousin. Also keep in mind that the heftier the pewter, the better its quality.

The Egyptians and Romans were early pewter makers, and by the 1100s, religious articles such as chalices were customarily crafted from pewter in England. In the 1600s, pewter was being used more and more for secular purposes as the middle class grew.

Notice the open-work handles on these porringers all dating between 1788 and 1820.

Skinner Auctions, Inc.

During the mid-1700s, pewter was the "CorningWare" of its era because most ordinary kitchen and dining articles such as spoons, beer tankards and measuring cups were crafted from it.

In the early days of the Industrial Revolution, pewter manufacturing swiftly moved from hand to machine production. The adaptable alloy could easily be cast, molded, spun and cut into countless objects. Many shapes could be duplicated using the spinning process, which rotated a thin pewter plate rapidly on a lathe to give it the shape of the wooden core. The metal could also be cast into flat pieces, then rolled in thin sheets and hammered into various articles. Hollowware such as teapots were made by casting the various pieces in molds, soldering them together and, finally, hand tooling them to smooth the seam marks.

This simple yet elegant plate was crafted in Providence, Rhode Island, between 1774 and 1809.

Skinner Auctions, Inc

British and Yankee Pewter

English pewter, so known for quality, usually had a touch mark akin to the hallmark or trademark of the silversmith. British pieces had to be marked, but in America no such law existed.

Thomas Bumstead of Boston began his career in 1654, and soon other Americans followed, giving Britain much competition. Between 1700 and 1850, approximately 200 American craftsmen created everything from tankards to porringers and plates.

Since the Brits supposedly labeled every piece, the tendency is to regard all unmarked pewter as American. That can be misleading because a few American examples were also labeled, while not every British item actually was marked, even though it was supposed to be.

The American Eagle

One celebrated American touch mark dating from the 1790s was the eagle. This popular motif was the symbol of our early federal government. The great names in American pewter are Danforth, Boardman, Melville, Sellew and the firm of Flagg & Homan.

Britannia

An updated formula for pewter dating from the mid-1700s became known as Britannia. This alloy lacked lead, whose harmful traits had been discovered. This new version used by the Brits and Yanks also adapted easily to machine production. In addition, Britannia was sometimes called white metal because it resembled silver more than the leaded version did.

Skinner Auctions, Inc.

Notice the mark of Thomas Danforth III of Stepney, Connecticut, who made this deep dish around 1790.

Mr. Wedgwood, Mr. Spode and Others Take Over

Ceramics contributed to pewter and Britannia's downfall by creating insurmountable competition. In the late 1700s and early 1800s, thanks to Staffordshire legends Wedgwood, Spode and others, fine china became reasonably priced for the first time in history. In addition, ceramics didn't tarnish and were more hygienic because they were easier to clean. Another bonus was that dishes came in sparkling colors. Ho-hum pewter had an uphill battle against blue and white and other venerated color combinations enhancing crockery!

Then another challenger arrived that was even more overwhelming than Staffordshire china. Modern electroplating, the process of

Skinner Auctions, Inc.

Around 1825, Hartford, Connecticut, artisans Boardman and Hart made this pint mug.

coating silver over a less expensive metal, had been perfected in the 1840s. The metallic veneering created a sterling silver look-alike without the expense. Victorians, always so tied to the latest trends, preferred silver plate over lackluster pewter counterparts. Thus, while pewter was an initial success of the Industrial Revolution, it became an early victim.

During the late 1800s and early 1900s, pewter faded out, except for use in religious articles such as chalices and crucifixes. When the antiquing craze exploded in the United States, collectors discovered antique pewter, which led to a mini renaissance for pewter making. In the 1920s, as Grand Rapids firms copied earlier furniture styles, pewter reproduction also blossomed. Today, these well made Flapper versions have matured into affordable semi-antiques. When you see the word "pewter" on the underside of a piece, that usually indicates 20th century manufacture. Remember that the more information on an item, the younger it is. How true this is concerning pewter. The Stieff Pewter Company leaves no doubt with its "Authentic Williamsburg Reproduction" mark.

Skinner Auctions, Inc.

Timothy Boardman made this beaker in New York City between 1822 and 1824.

To Polish or Not to Polish: That is the Question

By now you may be asking if tarnished pewter should be polished. Although it's customary to buff smudged silver, the question of what to do with less-than-sparkling pewter is controversial, to say the least. This longstanding dispute can split antiquing pals, so I'll let you answer this subjective question for yourself. Do you prefer shiny pewter, which testifies to spotless housekeeping? Or do you like pewter to proudly show its age? Pro-polishers assert that because pewter was

originally shiny, it should be kept that way. Anti-polishers, on the other hand, believe that the dull look showing age adds class and distinction. The choice is yours. Just avoid polishing too much, which could scratch the soft pewter surface. If you want the tarnish to remain, just keep dust rags handy to keep the "the kiss of time" from becoming "the kiss of grime."

Du Mouchelle's Auction

No doubt milk tasted all the better for the young child sipping from this early 1800s mug.

Chapter 27

Glass: A Clear Choice for Antiquers

Even in the 21st century, despite the mammoth escalation in prices for other antiques, glass remains quite affordable. From the 1800s through the 1960s, glass factories produced huge quantities of fine glassware, which is good news for us collectors.

The recipe for glass is silica (sand), soda and lime. Adding soda to sand lowers the temperature needed for glass production. Lime acts as a stabilizer, and additional oxides in the molten mixture produce colors. Formulas have remained basically unchanged since classical times.

Glass Through the Ages

By melting sand and other ingredients at more than 2,500 degrees Fahrenheit, ancient Egyptians created a fluid that could be formed into various objects while molten that hardened into permanent shapes after cooling.

The Greeks and Romans became expert glassmakers, but it wasn't until the Middle Ages that one Italian city became forever associated with fine glass. By the 1500s, Venice had become the premier glass center of the world, especially nearby Murano Island, within view of famous San Marco Cathedral.

While Venetians were crafting fine household articles, glass art-

The shades in this five-light chandelier were made by Steuben in the Gold Aurene line in the early 1900s.

Early Auction Company

Early Auction Company

**Look at these silver lids and cut bases to verify that the marriage
of cut glass and sterling silver created beautiful antiques.**

ists in other countries created stained glass window masterpieces for European churches. These religious works of art inspired worshipers just as those in Sainte Chappelle Church in Paris still do today.

By the early 1600s, secret glass formulas escaped Venice and entered France. (My cherished France does indeed have a history of "borrowing" artistic ideas from the Italians.) In time, the techniques arrived in two future glass centers, England and Bohemia.

By the 1600s, competing European makers fabricating household articles lessened the demand for Venetian glass. But miraculously, during the late 1800s, Venice made a comeback, and today famous Murano, still located on the nearby island, is more popular than ever. Murano pieces are fine examples of future antiques.

Production Methods

The best way to master glass is to carefully study production processes, since classification is based on these methods. The major groups are blown, mold-blown, pressed and molded glass.

Blown Glass

Before modern times, the traditional method for making glass pieces was air blowing. The glass ingredients were first heated to a semiliquid consistency. Next, the glassblower dipped a blowing iron—a long hollow pipe with a protective wooden mouthpiece—into molten glass to collect a small glob on the tip called a gather. Then he blew through the tube to expand the glass to the desired size. After briefly cooling, he rolled the mixture, still attached to the rod, over a heavy metal or marble surface to flatten the base. A final blowing of the semi-molten glass was the last step for shaping. As the glass was broken from the rod, a mark, called a pontil, was left on the bottom. This spot resembles a circular scar or what I call a "belly button."

Early Auction Company

Mold-Blown Glass

The Industrial Revolution improved glass manufacturing by creating faster and less labor-intensive methods. The first step towards modernization arrived in 1826 when an American mechanic developed mold-blown glass. Molten glass on the tip of the rod was inserted into a three-dimensional mold with hinged parts. Air was blown into the tube, forcing the molten glass to the sides. Molds with indentations created designs similar to the way a cookie press forms a gingerbread man. As the molten mixture cooled, the hinged sides were opened, and the resulting object, such as a goblet or bowl, was removed.

Mount Washington made this kerosene lamp in the late 1800s. After the premiere of *Gone With the Wind* in 1939, this lamp and similar models resembling those in the film were forever known by the movie's name.

Identifying a mold-blown piece is simple because of the seams that remain. Bases of stemmed goblets, for example, have obvious mold marks. The mold-blown process significantly speeded up glass production, increasing supplies and reducing prices.

Pressed Glass

The pressed glass process is an even faster and less expensive production method. The process debuted at a fortuitous time, as the fervor for bric-a-brac soon reached it peak.

Pressed glass was first made around 1827 in Cambridge and Sandwich, Massachusetts. The technique eliminated the need for lungpower because a plunger forced molten glass into a mold. With pressed-glass pieces, patterns were always on the outside, while interiors remained smooth, regardless of the depth of the designs.

The Sandwich firm hoped to create a less expensive version of costly multi-faceted cut glass. But something quite unexpected occurred. Sandwich glass resembled lace rather than cut glass. These 1830s pieces are still called "lacy glass," with such prized designs as American eagles and Yankee clipper ships. Spotting examples is straightforward, since its pet name defines its appearance. This revolutionary fabrication worked best with pieces that were relatively low, such as 2-inch high bowls and one very captivating example.

Glass cup plates, resembling small saucers, were made between 1800 and 1850. These little treasures, usually 3 to 4 inches in diameter, provide an intriguing insight into old-time customs. A cup plate held a teacup, while the more standard saucer had another function that may surprise you. Since teeth were usually in a precarious state before modern dentistry, very hot beverages were wisely avoided. During the days of primitive cooking equipment, scorching tea or coffee was poured into the larger saucer for cooling. The less scalding beverage was savored from the saucer, which, of course, was deeper than modern versions. (A cavernous saucer usually indicates age, as it also does for the matching teacup.) The cup plate was the precursor to the modern coaster used to protect tablecloths or wooden surfaces. The Boston and Sandwich Glass Company also produced eye-catching glass handles that added panache to country sewing tables and chests of drawers.

Pairpoint painted the scene on the inside of the glass shade so it could be viewed from the outside.

Early Auction Company

Molded Glass

The pressed method, once perfected, revolutionized glass making the world over. By the time Victoria became Queen of England in 1837, England, Germany and France were using Yankee high-tech methods to produce lower cost items. Although molded glass was made essentially the same way as pressed glass, larger molds were used

Early Auction Company

Tiffany also crafted Favrile glass in blue. Notice the swirling ribbed body in true Art Nouveau spirit.

Early Auction Company

Early Auction Company

The base of this Tiffany lily lamp is bronze, and the shades are Favrile glass. The base is stamped "Tiffany Studios New York 319."

Tiffany captured Art Nouveau's flowing lines in this glorious floriform vase from the early 1900s.

to create bowls, pitchers and compotes (large bowls on stands). By the Civil War, three-fourths of all glass objects crafted in America were made by the pressed or molded method. Although pressed and molded glass are fundamentally the same, in antiquese pressed glass usually indicates earlier pieces such as charming Sandwich glass cup plates, while molded glass signifies Victorian or 20th century origin.

Art Glass

As factories produced an increasing amount of glass in the late 1800s, several highly talented artisans returned to traditional ways of hand-crafting magnificent glass. Art glass was handmade blown glass and became a major artifact of the Arts and Crafts movement that celebrated the rebellion against machinery discussed in the furniture section. Mssrs. Tiffany, Majorelle and Gallé, all Art Nouveau superstars, were less than thrilled with factory-made glass.

Depression Glass

The horrendous Great Depression is mostly forgotten, especially by younger generations. But today, the most famous product of those scary times reveals the positive power of antiques. All these years later, the Depression has practically become synonymous with a beloved, inexpensive brightly colored glass lovingly called Depression glass.

Depression glass was mass produced from the 1920s to World War II. Coming in all the jubilant hues popular during Art Deco Days, colors included green, pink, blue, red, amber and white. Federal, Jeanette, and Hocking Glass were famous firms.

How this glass earned its name is a slice of Amer-

Don't you want to caress this Amberina water pitcher from the late 1800s?

Early Auction Company

ican history. As the Depression ravaged business during the 1930s, companies employed various imaginative gimmicks for increasing sales. One in particular was enormously successful. The brainstorm worked something like 1950s trading stamps. When customers bought gas or saw a film, they were given a free piece of inexpensive glass such as a bowl or plate as a bonus. Imagine how seeing a film with Greta Garbo or Barbara Stanwyck plus getting a free glass bowl must have lifted spirits!

Heisey, Cambridge and Fostoria

Upscale molded glass dating from the 1920s and 1930s can easily be confused with Depression glass. Although glass from Heisey and Cambridge (both of Ohio) and Fostoria (of West Virginia) were also mass produced, they were higher quality and were sold in department stores rather than given out as "freebies."

The Heisey Company crafted fine pieces between 1896 and 1957. Most Heisey was marked with an "H" inside a diamond, but sometimes the company glued on paper labels that eventually fell off. Heisey has a thick design with a heavy feel and usually features a bottom displaying a fluted design radiating from the center.

Cambridge is another quality glass created between 1901 and 1954 in the town with the same name. A "C" inside a triangle was the mark that appeared on the underside of etched ice buckets and cocktail shakers.

Fostoria opened in 1887 in Fostoria, Ohio, and later moved to Moundsville, West Virginia. The firm is still making quality, yet reasonably priced glassware, usually marked "Fostoria."

Decorating Glass

How glass is decorated provides another method of identification. The primary examples are cut, etched, engraved, painted and stenciled.

CUT GLASS

Cut glass is the most radiant glass ever to bedeck dining rooms. Just watch the rays of the sun shining through the many faceted cuttings of a bowl or tumbler to savor such luminous artistry. Identifying cut glass is as simple as caressing a bowl or compote to feel the sharp edges of this high-end antique. Although imitation cut glass resembles the real McCoy, the imitation is much friendlier to your fingertips.

Antique cut glass is quite heavy due to a special ingredient. In 1676, Englishman George Ravenscroft devised a breakthrough formula of adding lead to molten glass. This kept cooled glass from breaking as designs were cut. Objects were first shaped by mouth blowing, then a metal or stone wheel was used to cut motifs in the glass.

No grand Victorian party was complete without a cut-glass punch bowl.

The English, Scots, Irish and Czechs have crafted first-rate cut glass for centuries, and I am happy to report that they are still doing so. Ireland is known for Waterford, Scotland for Stuart, England for Tudor, and the Czech Republic for numerous fine firms.

Since cut glass resembles quartz rock crystal, it sometimes is called crystal because "crystal" is more elegant sounding than "glass." This appealing misnomer mirrors the more infamous "china or porcelain" debate. To set the record straight, the term "crystal" properly belongs

These cut-glass goblets from the American Brilliant period were quite heavy, even when empty.

to the mineral, while the word "glass" refers to the product formed by melting silica and other chemicals.

America made fabulous cut glass between 1880 and 1915 during the golden age of American cut glass so charmingly called "The Brilliant Period." Most pieces aren't signed, so spotting a signature is a little like learning to ride a bike. Mastering the skill can be tricky but once you know how, you will never forget. Take cut glass outside during a sunny day and turn it while searching for a signature. Magnifying glasses are a real help; in fact, they are so helpful that I suggest you make a pair part of your antiquing equipment. On a big fruit bowl, the mark is usually on bottom. Though names are tough to spot, once you find the first, others will be easier. Don't be disappointed if you don't find a signature, because most cut glass was unsigned. Some famous names are Libby, Clark, Hawkes, Tuthil, Sterling Cut Glass, and Hoare.

To distinguish between old and modern cut glass, just let your hands do the caressing. Contemporary is duller because pieces are acid-dipped to remove sharp edges. While engraved and etched glass are somewhat similar to cut glass, engraved and etched glassware have shallower designs than their cut glass cousins.

ENGRAVED GLASS

Engraved glass patterns are created by pressing small spinning copper discs coated with emery powder and oil against the glass to form intricate designs. Before engravers used copper wheels, they relied on diamonds to cut designs. Because engraved designs are not as deep as those in cut glass, this process was ideal for monogramming stemware.

ETCHED GLASS

Etching uses hydrofluoric acid to decorate glass. The undecorated parts of a glass piece are coated with wax and a design is scratched onto the remaining unwaxed areas. After the wax has dried, hydrofluoric acid attacks the unprotected parts, carving designs into the glass.

Antique glass is magnificent, thanks to its beauty, and so many have friendly prices. If you're considering collecting antiques, you can't go wrong with glass, whatever variety pleases you.

SECTION FOUR

Antiques Legends

Chapter 28

Wedgwood: A 1700s Achiever

While Thomas Chippendale was fashioning mahogany masterpieces in the years preceding the American Revolution, another Englishman, Josiah Wedgwood (1730-1795), was creating ceramic works of art. Today Wedgwood's breathtaking innovations grace museum collections all over the world. To me, he is the "Chippendale" of the china industry, and his reputation in his field remains second-to-none.

Wedgwood was born in 1730 in the Staffordshire region of central England, the same area you read about in the ceramics chapter. As you now know, Staffordshire is to English china what Detroit once was to American automobiles. Wedgwood was the youngest of 13 children in a poor family, but by his death in 1795, this incomparable achiever was a millionaire who had revolutionized the ceramics business. But besides his numerous accomplishments, he was also a loving husband and father and man of unquestionably high character.

This genius followed family tradition by going into the then rather primitive pottery trade. The technological advances of the Industrial Revolution had not yet affected Staffordshire firms, so almost everything was still handmade. As you recall, many articles in the 1700s were shaped on ancient potter's wheels. An artisan pumped a foot pedal to turn the heavy wheel. As the disk spun, the potter skillfully shaped the wet clay into useful articles.

Wedgwood, however, faced a difficult problem. When he was just 12 years old, he contracted smallpox, which left him with a constantly infected right knee. It seemed impossible for him to enter a trade that demanded the ability to constantly pump a foot peddle, so his prospects in the china business seemed dismal. Fortunately, he was determined to succeed. As a true achiever, he transformed a liability into an asset. Instead of throwing clay on the wheel, he focused on manufacturing and perfecting designs. Like fellow countryman Chippendale, Wedgwood perfectly blended business acumen with artistic

Skinner Auctions, Inc.

A Jasperware portrait medallion of Queen Charlotte, who started Wedgwood on the road to success. The piece was made by the Wedgwood firm, circa 1779.

skills, which eventually propelled him to legendary status in the antiques world.

To fully appreciate the significance of his career, let's review a few of his many accomplishments. Before his day, only the very wealthy could afford china, so his first distinction was to make inexpensive, yet quality everyday dishes. His middle-of-the-road ceramic (which is still being made today) was elevated to royal status when christened "Queensware" in honor of Queen Charlotte, the wife of George III, who bought a set. Such clever advertising kept him ahead of competitors.

Although a small-town lad, this potter knew he would have to move to London to make it big in his field. In August 1768, with the help of his beloved partner Thomas Bentley, he opened a showroom to cater to the rich and famous. He established his reputation by selling china services to aristocracy and the fashionable set. He sold his wares to some of the most prestigious clients in the world. The Empress Catherine of Russia, for example, bought a 1,000 piece set that is now displayed in Saint Petersburg, Russia.

Although he enjoyed many successes, his greatest masterpiece would forever be linked with his name. In 1774, after fours years and thousands of experiments, he perfected a unique blue and white porcelain that brought him everlasting fame and fortune. Neoclassical Jasperware (named after the stone called jasper) was decorated with white two-dimensional Grecian figures on the cherished blue background that eventually took his name. Jasperware has remained so beloved that it is still being crafted in the 21st century.

He was not only a kind and generous employer, but also an activist for human rights. Long before it was politically chic to oppose slavery, he was an abolitionist. In fact some Jasperware was crafted depicting

Here's a wonderful example of Jasperware with the famous Wedgwood blue.

The neoclassical style of this Jasperware plaque was a perfect complement to Hepplewhite and Sheraton furniture.

a slave asking the poignant question, "Am I not a man and a brother?" No doubt this artistic triumph and political statement helped end slavery in the British Empire long before the Emancipation Proclamation was issued in the United States.

Besides all his grand achievements, we Americans should revere him for two special reasons. Yankee patriots constantly complained about the imbalance of trade between colonists and their mother country, but our antiques champion was an exception. In the 1760s, five tons of white clay exported from the mountains of western North Carolina near the present town of Highlands arrived at his Staffordshire facility.

Although a loyal British subject to King George III (how could he be anything else when the Queen was his client?), he was discreetly pro-Yankee during the American Revolution. Ever the good businessman, he thought citizens of an independent and prosperous country would be able to buy even more of his china. Rumor claims that he put his china where his mouth was. His faith in the American cause was so great that commemorative pieces glorifying American heroes

Skinner Auctions, Inc.

These black basalt pieces date from the late 1800s. such as George Washington were being crafted even before America actually won.

Our legend even had renown descendents. Perhaps you have read the theories of evolution written by his grandson, Charles Darwin? As for the man himself, his designs from the mid-1700s are still being made in the 21st century, confirming an enduring genius. Quite a series of accomplishments for a youngster born into poverty and afflicted with small pox! (Incidentally, he had his bad leg amputated in his late 30s and was fitted with a fine wooden replacement. As soon as he recovered, he went right back to work.)

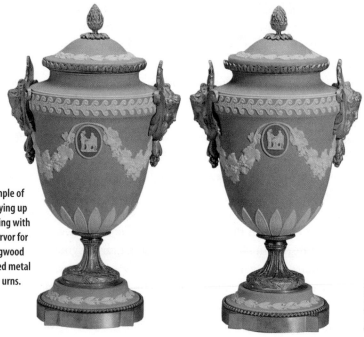

Here's an example of Wedgwood staying up to date. In keeping with the Victorian fervor for gold, the Wedgwood firm added gilded metal to these 1882 urns.

Skinner Auctions, Inc.

Skinner Auctions, Inc.

The Wedgwood pottery produced these Art Deco pieces during the 1920s and 1930s.

Whenever china crafted during his reign or by his descendants is mentioned, no grandiose adjectives are needed to convey quality, beauty and timelessness. Just the name "Wedgwood" says it all. By the way, if you ever visit the Wedgwood center near Stoke-on-Trent in England, you'll learn a great deal of useful information. The wonderful people at Wedgwood continue the master's gentility and, like their first boss, are fond of Americans.

After seeing the Wedgwood Museum, take time to visit the elegantly understated tomb of Josiah and his beloved wife, Sarah, in the Stoke cemetery. When I brought them flowers, I asked Mr. Wedgwood if my pup could be named in his honor and if he would consent to becoming the patron saint of antiquers. All these years later, I have to tell you that during his 16 years, my dog Josiah lived up to his stellar namesake.

One final tip about this antiques superstar: Wedgwood gives us a humorous bonus. The name "Wedgwood" has only one "e." When you spot Wedgwood spelled with two "e's," enjoy a chuckle (silently of course, as it's unwise to point out the goof and make enemies). Remember, antiques and a good sense of humor go well together and make life so much more enjoyable.

Chapter 29

Three Cheers for the Ladies!

I would like to do away with a tendency toward certain generalizations concerning antiques. The first is that only ladies were trendsetters in the world of antiques. While women were the primary movers and shakers, they didn't have exclusive influence over the fashion world. It's true that the following women created a lasting impact on antiques: Queen Anne, Queen Victoria, and the American colonies' last official queen, Charlotte, who was the wife of George III. Also, the French empress Josephine made the Empire style quite chic as her husband Bonaparte tried to conquer Europe. Later, in the mid-1800s, her granddaughter-in-law Eugénie brought Rococo Revival to the public eye. And of course, there were the two American sovereigns of panache, First Lady Mary Todd Lincoln and fictional Scarlet O'Hara, who both tried to "Rococoize" America in the mid-1800s.

To set the record straight, however, you should know that a few gentlemen also influenced the public's fancy. For instance, George IV, whom I affectionately call "Regency George," brought Josephine's Empire style to Britain to anger his father, George III, who loathed Napoleon. The Regency era would have been somewhat bland without the French accoutrements he made so trendy. In addition, we Yanks have Thomas Jefferson, who brought lovely French artifacts and customs to America. His guests at Monticello enjoyed fine French wine and slept in beds built in alcoves, a design the third President copied from the French. So now you know that men as well as women were fashion setters.

Another stereotype suggests that women never participated in business affairs. The highly successful gents Hepplewhite, Sheraton, Spode, Chippendale and Wedgwood did indeed appear to control the furniture and china fields, but not totally. Mr. Wedgwood often gave his beloved wife, Sarah, credit for her good business sense. I can almost hear Mrs. Wedgwood saying, "No, Josiah, better stick to the blue and white. Women like that more."

Mrs. Hepplewhite also had a hand in business affairs. As you remember, after the furniture designer died, his wife continued publishing her husband's design book with great success. Thanks to her, those stellar square-tapered legs grace many pieces of antique furniture.

Finally, when experts discuss the best English silversmiths of any century, Hester Bateman (1708-1794) is usually listed in the top five. Yes, indeed, this enormously venerated silversmith was a lady. After the death of her husband, Hester ran the family's silver business, making it even more prosperous, which wasn't an easy feat for a woman in those days. Her silver, from spoons to teapots, followed the neoclassical Hepplewhite and Sheraton furniture styles and looked magnificent next to any piece of Wedgwood. When you visit museums, you can easily spot her teapots because they're usually helmet shaped with engraved Roman urns, reflecting their neoclassical characteristics.

Critics assert that Mrs. Bateman could neither read nor write. If true, that in my opinion, just adds more clout to her astonishing resumé. Even without a formal education, she made her silver legendary. Her son, Jonathan, took over when she retired at 82. Her grand-

Hester Bateman captured the neoclassical design to perfection when she created this teapot between 1787 and 1788.

son, representing the third generation of the Bateman legacy, joined the firm in 1805. A good businessperson who followed his grandma's savvy example, he adapted his work to public demand. He left the neoclassical taste so perfected by Mrs. Bateman and created the lavish Rococo Revival pieces then in demand.

Hester Bateman remains an incomparable artist of any country or century. She was not only a museum-quality silversmith, but also a role model of success. Mesdames Bateman, Wedgwood and Hepplewhite show us that in the old days women had more say in business than currently acknowledged.

Forsythes' Auctions

Silver making firms in the early 20th century reproduced the neoclassical lines of the 1700s Bateman original silver pieces.

Chapter 30

Currier and Ives: The Rodgers and Hammerstein of Antiques

For many Broadway and Hollywood aficionados, one dazzling duo is considered far superior to the rest. Just as Rodgers and Hammerstein were famous for wonderful musicals, Currier and Ives are second-to-none for antique American prints. For nearly 50 years in the 1800s, these two men recorded both historical and everyday events in the United States. Today their works are highly cherished antiques.

Nathaniel Currier was born in Roxbury, Massachusetts, on March 27, 1813. At 15, he started on the road to immortality by apprenticing in the Boston print shop of William and John Pendleton. Currier learned lithography, the then high-tech process that would catapult him to fame and fortune.

Lithography was a crucial player in the Industrial Revolution. In 1798, Aloys Senefelder of Bavaria devised a process that sped up picture making while reducing costs. The technique is based on the principle that water and oil don't mix. To create a colored lithograph, a drawing was first made with a greasy crayon on a flat limestone. The stone was moistened with water, then a coat of ink was applied with a roller. The greasy crayon lines held the ink but repelled the water. Finally, paper was placed on the stone and picked up ink from the greasy lines, thereby reproducing the original drawing. Coloring was done by hand, much the same way paint-by-number pictures are created today.

In 1835, Currier went solo and produced various works marked "N. Currier, Lithographer." He created portraits, disaster scenes and memorial prints and sold them in front of his shop. Before the widespread use of photography, Currier's work filled the same niche that television does today. The famous "Ruins of the Planter's Hotel, New

"American Country Life: October Afternoon," 1855, created by Mr. Currier before the arrival of Mr. Ives.

Orleans," was an early success, and in 1840 Currier hit the jackpot with the "Awful Conflagration of the Steamboat Lexington in Long Island Sound." Since newspapers in the 1800s rarely included illustrations, this work became an instant hit for a curious public eager to visualize the catastrophe.

Currier's star continued to rise when James Merritt Ives (1824-1895), a native New Yorker, became Currier's bookkeeper in 1852. Ives streamlined production and in 1857 became a partner. Currier & Ives was launched, and the rest is antiques history.

Currier & Ives operated at 33 Spruce Street in Manhattan. The third floor contained printing presses, while the fourth held artists who did original drawings. The fifth housed colorists, who were usually immigrant girls from Germany. Each artist added a single color to a print, then passed it on for the next color. Everyone worked from a master print to guarantee accuracy, and a touch-up expert checked for quality. During the Civil War, demand for prints depicting battles became

"American Farm Scenes, No. 1," 1853, another work by Mr. Currier before the arrival of Mr. Ives.

so great that coloring stencils were developed to speed up production. Some black and white Currier & Ives prints were sold to schools, where students following the firm's instructions learned the art of coloring.

The successful partners described their business as "Publishers of Cheap and Popular Pictures" and produced an enormous number of prints. Between 1835 and 1907, the firm produced more than 7,500 different titles with a total of over a million prints, ranging from 3 by 5 inches to 18 by 27 inches. Historical lithographs such as "Washington's Reception" were very popular. Of course, the tragedies of the Civil War created many topics for Currier & Ives to record for posterity, such as the "Battle of Gettysburg" and "Night by the Camp Fire." Disasters had a huge following, and the 1871 "The Burning of Chicago" was a big money maker. Other popular subjects were sentimental themes so esteemed by Victorians. Particularly liked were the American Homestead series, which depicted the American home during changes of the four seasons.

Currier retired in 1880, while Ives remained active until his death in 1895. Chauncey, the eldest son of Ives, gained control from Curri-

"The Farmer's Home-Autumn," 1864, by Currier & Ives. Victorians loved such sentimentality. Note that the gilded frame is original and looks antique in a lovely way.

Skinner Auctions, Inc.

er's son, but in 1907 he closed the business because modern photography was too competitive.

Today, Currier & Ives are synonymous for fine prints depicting a vanished America. Many reprints of Currier & Ives have been made in the 20th century. Always examine a potential Currier & Ives purchase out of its frame. Look in the lower left or right corner to check for any tiny print that may indicate whether it is genuine or reproduction. You will usually find information about being republished. In the 1930s and 1940s, insurance companies often reprinted Currier & Ives lithographs for calendars.

The most delightful part of collecting genuine Currier & Ives prints is that they are still affordable. To get the most for your antiques budget, pick sentimental titles. A letter-sized "Anna Marie" from 1849 usually retails for about $175. Well-known historic scenes cost much more, such as the famous 1840 print of the Lexington, which often sells for $4,000. Currier & Ives will stylishly endure the test of time because they vividly capture the nostalgia of America long ago.

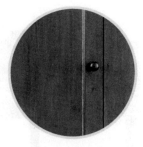

Chapter 31
The Shakers: No Nonsense Practicality

Time and fate can create quite unforeseen yet superb legacies when it comes to antiques. When Ann Lee, the leader of the Society of Believers in Christ's Second Appearance, left England in 1774 for the American colonies, religion, not furnishings was her objective. Her followers settled in Watervliet, near Albany, New York, and in time became known as Shakers because they shook or danced during religious services. By the 1840s, about 6,000 members had settled in Maine, Vermont, Ohio, Rhode Island and Kentucky.

How amazed Ann Lee would be to know that today the term "Shaker" is more commonly known for its association with antiques than for religious principles. However, the beautiful furnishings created by Shakers have emerged as their greatest champion by piquing collectors interest in Shaker beliefs. Thus, their wonderful cherry tables and maple rocking chairs have helped to spread their philosophies of pacifism and equality of the sexes.

Shaker furniture had a very practical beginning. When the Shakers first arrived in the infant United States in the 1790s, they

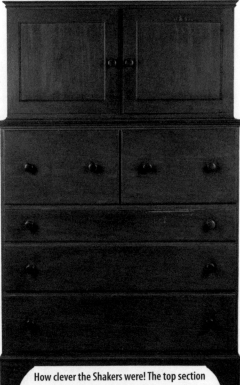

How clever the Shakers were! The top section of this 1840 piece is a cupboard, while the lower area is a chest of drawers.

Skinner Auctions, Inc.

A one-drawer 1850 table has rounded legs of the Sheraton
style, but the tapering is pure Hepplewhite.

started crafting basic furniture such as chairs and tables for their im-
mediate needs, so furniture was made without adornments. Never
would a fancy curio cabinet be found in their settlements, because
Shakers concentrated on utilitarian pieces like sturdy tables.

The 1790s to the Civil War were the peak years for Shaker furniture, while lesser pieces were made as late as 1900. The Shakers prin-
cipally followed the lines of the Hepplewhite and Sheraton styles that
remained stylish in the mid-1800s. Locally grown woods, cherry and
walnut, were the most popular for sewing tables or work tables that
today are called nightstands. Some had the pleasing square tapered
legs first designed by Hepplewhite, while others followed Sheraton's
rounded version.

The saying, "Build a better mousetrap and the world will beat a
path to your door" is true when it comes to Shaker chairs. What originally had been a cottage industry grew into a factory system that
would have pleased even industrialist Henry Ford. The Mt. Lebanon,
New York, colony produced many chairs with a stenciled "Mt. Lebanon" label.

Chairs were undeniably the specialty of the Shakers and were sold
in nearby towns and villages. The slat back, or ladder back, was their
most successful chair. Thanks to those slats, these chairs could be

This circa 1800 pine cupboard with original red
paint wash is pure understated elegance.

hung on a wooden wall peg when not used. On each side of the back, an atttractive flame- or acorn-shaped finial added a little flair.

Another charming chair, the "tilter," was equipped with ball-and-socket feet on back legs. This novel invention allowed the sitter to tilt backwards without wearing down the back legs.

Shaker furniture, whether chests of drawers or candlestick stands, have a country look, since fancy carving or veneering rarely embel-

lished Shaker works. Such decorations were deemed unnecessary. This was quite radical in the mid-1800s when Victorian consumers relished flamboyant touches. Even in the 21st century, Shaker pieces seem as modern as though made yesterday. Others agreed, especially Gustav Stickley, who in the early 1900s gave much credit to the Shakers for inspiring his furniture designs known as Craftsman that was highlighted earlier.

Not only are Shaker antiques stunningly beautiful, they're packed with loving sentiments. Webb Garrison in his *Civil War Trivia and Fact Book* points out that although the Shakers were pacifists, they helped victims of both sides during the war. The members of Pleasant Hill, Kentucky, fed more than 50,000 Union and Confederate soldiers. That was rather a risky undertaking, since Kentucky was officially a Union state. Talk about getting antiques with terrific aura! Just imagine the warm vibrations from a Shaker piece that originated from that charming settlement.

Originally this pine cupboard could have been built into a wall.

Chapter 32

The First Ladies of Folk Art

In the late 1800s and early 1900s, the accepted philosophy among collectors was that antiques had to have a European pedigree to be considered first class. Consequently, artifacts created in the United States were rarely (if ever) considered top drawer. Of course, several pioneers such as the great Wallace Nutting, mentioned in Chapter 16, opposed this viewpoint. Antiquers, and especially aficionados of Folk Art, owe much applause to two collectors whom I call "The First Ladies of Folk Art." Besides putting Folk Art on the antiques map, these savvy antiquers demonstrated that an American heritage was just as good as a European lineage.

Before you have the delight of meeting our First Ladies of Folk Art, let's define the unique area of antiques they so relished. A Folk Art piece is a handmade object created by an untrained or informally taught artisan from any country. The one universal trait folk artists of all eras and all nationalities share is a lack of official schooling. For example, folk painters did not attend art academies to study portraiture, and folk furniture makers seldom apprenticed under cabinetmakers. A folk artist could have been a girl practicing her stitching on a sampler during the 1820s or a vagabond trading carvings for food during the Depression.

Folk Art pieces dating before 1920 are genuine antiques, as we discussed in Chapter 1. More recent examples from the Depression, such as woodcarvings, are semi-antiques/collectibles. And, of course, handmade quilts from the Reagan era are now known as Retro Folk Art.

To Each His/Her Own in Pursuit of Folk Art

Urban antiques such as furniture and silver can be specifically classified by styles to establish pedigree, but no such rules exist for Folk

Art. Remember, what constitutes Folk Art is merely in the eye of the beholder. So what your antiques coach considers Folk Art, you may call trash (or perhaps vice-versa). This individualistic philosophy opens a tremendous door for collecting at bargain prices.

Now that you have a clear grasp of the general guidelines for Folk Art, you will fully appreciate the challenges our First Ladies of Folk Art faced during their antiquing adventures.

Abby Aldrich Rockefeller (1874-1948) was married to John D. Rockefeller, Jr. of the Standard Oil fortune. With all that money, we might think her life was a collector's Technicolor fantasy. However, Bernice Kert, in her splendid book *Abby Aldrich Rockefeller: the Woman in the Family* reveals that this was not so. Her husband constantly voiced his disapproval of her selections. Conservative Mr. Rockefeller preferred centuries-old antiques with European pedigrees such as French tapestries. Don't get the wrong impression of him, however; he was a wonderful philanthropist who gave millions for the restoration of Williamsburg, Virginia, and the Palace of Versailles in France.

While Mr. R. was a traditionalist, Mrs. R. eagerly sought Folk Art carvings of American eagles, among other things. Today, tourists visiting the enchanting Colonial Williamsburg can also tour the Rockefeller home, Bassett Hall. Abby's collection of weather vanes, chalk ware and samplers are lovingly displayed in her memory.

Mrs. R. didn't limit her artistic endeavors just to Folk Art; she was one of the founders of the Museum of Modern Art in New York City. That was pretty heroic for the 1930s, when most critics thought Folk Art and modern art belonged in the city dump. Having such diverse tastes also reveals her self-confidence, which is essential for a contented collector.

Electra Havemeyer Webb

Our second First Lady of Folk Art, Electra Havemeyer Webb (1888-1960), was the daughter of Louisine and Harry Havemeyer. Her parents were famous New York collectors of works by Degas, Manet, Renoir and Cassatt. The next time New York City beckons, take time to see their paintings displayed at the Metropolitan Museum of Art.

Did Electra follow in her parents' collecting footsteps? Hardly! In the spirit of her highly individualistic name, Electra pursued the beat of her own antiques drummer. By the time she was 18, Electra was hooked on a special area of American antiques. She had little interest in fancy urban examples such as silver tea services by Paul Revere. Rather, she collected, or more accurately stockpiled, articles that were considered rubbish. One of her early purchases was a carved wooden figure of a Native American. This prime example of Folk Art from the 1800s, commonly called a cigar store Indian, was a three-dimensional sign advertising a tobacco shop.

Electra's mother, whose collecting tastes were more in tune with Mr. Rockefeller's, was absolutely aghast at Electra's collection. She reputedly confronted her daughter with the comment, "You who have been brought up on Renoir and Degas, how can you collect such trash?" But that question didn't intimidate the self-assured Electra. In fact, in 1947 in Shelburne, Vermont, she created the Shelburne Museum, a tremendous resource for grateful collectors to learn about Folk Art.

Folk Art's endorsement by Abby Aldrich Rockefeller and Electra Havemeyer Webb marked the beginning of its graduation from junk to "museum quality." Just check the ground floor of one of my favorite places in the whole world to understand why these First Ladies of Folk Art are so dear. The Art Institute of Chicago in its American Gallery displays splendid examples such as country furniture and paintings.

Shortly before Mrs. Webb died, someone asked her how she defined Folk Art. Her reply: "Folk means people, which includes all of us. Therefore, folk art is the self-expression of art from the heart and hands of the people." Kudos to Mrs. Webb (and Mrs. Rockefeller)!

How Mrs. Webb would have loved this wooden tobacconist's figure, fondly known as a "cigar store Indian." Thomas V. Brooks (1825-1895) carved it in Chicago around 1880.

Skinner Auctions, Inc.

The artist of this watercolor, who depicted Lady Liberty in the late 1700s or early 1800s, was a fervent patriot.

Garth's Auctions, Inc.

Before looking at definitive examples, we need to consider one final point about Folk Art terminology. Through the years, some people have called antiques with a rustic or country flavor "primitive."

Folk/Naïve Art

Loomism

Never use the word primitive to describe Folk Art.

Primitive implies a lack of quality, and to me it is downright condescending. Fortunately, today that word is generally not used. Enough of the negative; let's look at another good phrase for these unique antiques. Naïve Art, the term used by the British and French, captures the informality or innocence of these artifacts. But who is your antiques coach to argue with the First Ladies of Folk Art? The choice is yours; use the term

"Folk Art" or follow our European collecting cousins by saying "Naïve Art." From now on, to be diplomatically and artistically correct, this primer will use both terms.

Here is your brief introduction to Folk/Naïve Art antiques. Always keep in mind that Folk/Naïve Art pieces can be from anywhere in the world. American Folk/Naïve Art pieces are important examples of Americana, which means American antiques.

Quilts

Quilts are my favorite example of Folk/Naïve Art. In the old days, frugal housewives saved every fabric scrap for quilt making. Designs were created by using the appliqué method

Garth's Auctions, Inc.

This wooden carving of a shoeshine boy and his female customer is entitled "It's a Shame to Take the Money." The power of innuendo!

of applying bits of fabric to a background material or by sewing small cloth pieces into a patchwork. Then the design was joined to a filler and background fabric with small stitching called quilting. The time-consuming methods remain the same today as in our great grandmother's day, with one exception. Around 1900, sewing machines made the task easier.

The colorful fabric pictures on quilts featured flowers, geometric designs and other motifs so cheerful and warming during frigid winter nights before central heat was available. There are more patterns than M & Ms in a pound bag. Designs include potted tulips on a white background and the classic multicolored concentric circles called the "Wedding Ring" pattern. The beauty and practicality of quilts justifiably guaranteed their popularity. No wonder succeeding generations regarded these practical and beautiful works of art as family heirlooms.

Three hooked rugs dating from 1880 to about 1925 are outstanding representatives of Folk/Naïve Art.

Skinner Auctions, Inc.

A superb sampler by Julia O'Brien depicting "Washington City, June the 4th 1812," two years before British troops marched into the capital.

Talk about a quilt with history! Skinner's catalogue says this quilt was made by a Ladies Auxiliary, whose members were mothers and sisters of men serving in the Union Army from Sandy Creek County, New York. It only has 34 stars because when it was begun in 1861, West Virginia and Nevada were not yet states.

Skinner Auctions, Inc.

A fine example of Folk/Naïve Art, this sampler was made in Rhode Island in 1789.

Paintings

Folk/Naïve Art paintings have been made with paint, pencil, ink, pastel, watercolor or chalk applied to a flat surface such as a board, canvas or even furniture. This genre, especially with scenes of children and pets has become very expensive. Paintings by Ammi Phillips (1788-1865) that seem almost one-dimensional have sold for hundreds of thousands of dollars. Bravo to this self-taught artist whose work was once so insensitively and inaccurately labeled "primitive." (Now I hope you agree about my aversion to this word.)

Sculpture

Sculpture includes three-dimensional objects made from clay, wood, stone or even cigar boxes. Mrs. Rockefeller's eagle and Mrs. Webb's cigar store Indians are two phenomenal examples. Wooden duck decoys and ship figureheads are other marvelous items that are routinely displayed in museums.

In the last decade, Tramp Art has become eagerly collected, which, of course, means higher prices. European immigrants brought this self-taught art to the United States. Most pieces dating from the 1860s to 1940s were made from wooden cigar boxes and were carved with pocket knives into everything from frames to boxes.

A glorious Folk/Naïve Art painting, circa 1830-1840. Notice the parlor, carpet, window overlooking a river, and the young lady's adoring calico cat.

Harry Remick, who painted this Kittery, Maine, house in 1868, may not have studied in Paris, but he was an excellent artist.

Furniture

Country furniture has become even trendier in the last few years. However, the expression "country furniture" has become almost trite and conjures images of crudely made wooden pieces with cut-out hearts and painted ducks. So let's use the term "Folk/Naïve Art furniture" for pieces crafted by informal furniture makers.

Folk/Naïve Art furniture is primarily utilitarian. For example, local woods such as cherry, walnut or pine were used for handcrafting plate racks so useful in the kitchen. When furniture makers followed Queen Anne or Chippendale styles, they produced far less exacting versions. Unlike city chairs, rural Chippendale chairs usually lacked ball-and-claw feet, since fine carving was usually learned by apprenticing to a cabinetmaker. Rarely will you find veneer on such pieces, and wood was usually at least an inch thick. Planks were never the same width, since timber was probably cut at home rather than at a lumberyard.

Folk/Naïve Art furniture was often painted with exuberant colors like yellow to brighten drab rooms. Pine was frequently decorated in a graining technique to resemble fancier oak or mahogany, while pieces crafted from various woods were given a uniform grain to make the pieces all appear to be from the same wood.

Rural folks never wasted anything. A homemade formula for paint, known as milk paint, used milk mixed with leftover eggs, coffee or even the blood of butchered animals. The blood from slaughtering created barn red, a glowing hue that was especially helpful for increasing visibility during heavy snow storms. As the Industrial Revolution progressed in the 1860s, inexpensive ready-made paints ended the use of milk paint.

My longtime friend and Lebanon, Ohio, antiques dealer Marilyn Haley, known for country antiques says, "It is often difficult to tell urban from country pieces." She warns to be careful of pieces that have been stripped of mahogany veneer. This has been known to happen to machine-made late-Empire pieces of the Pillar and Scroll era mentioned earlier to give them the "country look" of pine furniture. To be safe, buy from reputable retailers and make sure something like the phrase "rural origin" is included on your receipt to verify authenticity.

By the 1890s, a major product of the Industrial Revolution arrived in mail boxes all across America. The U.S. Postal Service delivered catalogues from the Chicago mail order firms Sears and Roebuck and Montgomery Ward. These companies offered mass-produced furniture far more affordable than homemade versions. By 1900, Folk/Naïve Art furniture was rarely made anymore because of the tremendous impact of the two Chicago businesses.

Remember our role models for collecting Folk/Naïve Art. Like Mrs. Rockefeller and Mrs. Webb, collect to the beat of your own antiques drummer, and you'll be a contented antiquer.

A montage of items dating from the late 1800s to the early 1900s, all examples of Tramp Art, a popular Folk Art style.

SECTION FIVE

Antiques Superstars

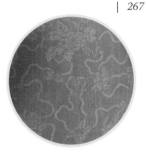

Chapter 33

Wing Chairs: Beauty and Comfort with a Hidden Agenda

Our word "chair" comes from the French "chaise." A chair is a moveable, individual piece of furniture consisting of a seat and backrest, with or without arms, that's usually supported on four legs.

A wide variety of chairs has been found in excavations or seen in wall paintings from ancient civilizations. As the Romans ruled Europe, they introduced chairs to their conquered subjects. Very little was recorded about these antiques until the late 1400s. In that century, designs of ponderous chairs, usually in oak or walnut, duplicated Gothic-looking arches as part of their design. Today, similar examples exist in churches.

By the 1400s and 1500s, chairs had acquired great status and were reserved for the heads of wealthy families. Although common folk used benches or stools, they weren't too deprived, since chairs were mostly squatty and terribly uncomfortable. By the time of Elizabeth I, chairs had become relatively common in nonaristocratic homes, and by the 1660s, they had become universal.

Of all household furnishings, chairs were usually the first to break or wear out, much the way teacups are the first to go in a set of china. Thus, the chair making trade was virtually a recession-proof business.

Styles and designs came and went throughout Europe and the Orient. Even as late as the 1600s, comfort, as we know it today, was not a priority. Chairs usually had stiff backs with tiny seats until the arrival of the most famous chair of all time changed everything.

The wing chair first appeared in the late 1600s during the reign of England's Charles II. The novelty was a blockbuster because it was far more comfortable than previous seating equipment. Thanks to an improved design developed in the early 1700s, wing chairs would never go out of fashion.

Around 1702, the Queen Anne style emerged in Britain. The design, named for the reigning monarch, was esteemed for its cabriole (or bow) legs, which as explained earlier, are knee legs with concave ankles. The Queen Anne style achieved its greatest success with a chair that would become an antiques icon.

These handsome pieces perfected under the Queen Anne style were totally upholstered except for their grand cabriole legs. As folklore has accurately taught, the celebrated wings had a mighty functional purpose. The clever, yet decorative elements helped keep drafts away from one's head in the days before central heating.

By the mid to late 1700s, wing chairs had achieved high status in the American colonies. At that time, an upholstered piece of furniture was very expensive because of costly fabric. It would be logical to assume that such a high-end piece would be proudly displayed in the parlor, but this wasn't the custom. Wing chairs were placed in bedrooms because they served another purpose, a really practical function revealing the ingenuity of our ancestors.

No doubt wing chairs were ideal places for reading and taking naps, but there was another important reason they were kept in the bedroom. Hidden discreetly under the seat cushion in most American versions was a

This period Queen Anne wing chair features trademark cabriole legs.

Skinner Auctions, Inc.

Du Mouchelle's Auction

Sometimes the only way to verify authenticity is to check the interior wooden structure of a chair, which has been done with this 1790s Hepplewhite wing chair.

chamber pot! Not only did wing chairs make trips to the outhouse unnecessary in the dark or during storms, they also kept the chamber pots warm. During the winter, a metal or china chamber pot not covered by a chair cushion would develop a glacially cold rim. So now you understand how Queen Anne style wing chairs successfully and stylishly combined beauty, utility and comfort.

Although the wing chair's discreet purpose has been replaced by modern plumbing (which proves there are indeed many advantages to living in the 21st century), these antique legends have remained ever chic. In the 1880s, furniture manufacturers started reproducing wing chairs, which are still made in the new millennium.

Here's one final delightful fact about the wing chair. Even more than 300 years after its debut, the ever-adaptable wing chair looks right at home next to a computer desk or wide-screen television.

Du Mouchelle's Auction

Ah, American ingenuity! This late-20th century wing chair made by the Ethan Allen firm is also a recliner.

Chapter 34

Rocking Chairs: Homegrown Furniture with Sway

Here's an antique that is as American as corn on the cob on the Fourth of July. Rocking chairs were invented right here in the United States around the time of the American Revolution. The credit for creating the first rocking chair has previously been accorded to the super patriot and Renaissance gentleman extraordinaire, Benjamin Franklin. More recent evidence, however, suggests that cabinetmaker William Savery (1721-1787) deserves the tribute. A bill dated 1774 from the celebrated Philadelphia cabinetmaker makes reference to adding rockers to an existing chair.

The earliest rocking chairs following Savery's alteration were stationary chairs with rockers added. Conversion was accomplished by notching the legs of a chair and fixing them to the rockers. In time, models were made that were designed as rocking chairs from the beginning rather than being converted from conventional chairs. These models relied on strong oak to bear the added strain on the legs and generally had wide wooden seats with a cushion for extra comfort.

In the first decade of the 1800s, a classic rocking chair emerged. The Boston rocker was an adaptation of the celebrated Windsor chair so cherished for its spindle backs and sides. The rolled seat—a main characteristic—curved inward, while the rear area scrolled upward. The Boston rocker, like its Windsor cousin, was often painted dark green or black.

Early rocking chairs were nicknamed "carpet cutters" because the repeated movement back and forth wore out hooked rugs and fine Persian carpets. By the mid-1800s, rocking chairs were manufactured in myriad sizes, with and without arms. Styles ranged from the superornate Rococo Revival of the 1850s to the more restrained Eastlake so popular in the 1870s. Even the religious Shakers crafted their own understated model in cherry or maple with, of course, the recognizable horizontal back bars known as "ladder backs."

An upholstered Rococo Revival version of this American invention acquired a President's name because of a tragic event. While Abraham Lincoln enjoyed a play at the Ford Theater in Washington, D.C. during an April evening in 1865, he sat in a Rococo Revival rocking chair. Ever since that catastrophic event, rocking chairs with tufted upholstery and carved curlicues resembling the Ford Theater original have become known as "Lincoln rockers."

Perhaps rocking chairs inspired William Morris, the legendary Arts and Crafts designer discussed previously. Just relax in a Morris chair with its incredible reclining back to appreciate the tranquil similarity between rocking chairs and the ancestor of modern recliners.

Rocking chairs continued to be made in many sizes and styles well into the 20th century. In the 1930s, Sears offered a mass-produced version with

This highly decorated rocking chair dates from the late 1800s or early 1900s.

These two cane-seat and cane-back rocking chairs date from just after the Civil War.

Jackson's International Auctions

Jackson's International Auctions

reddish mahogany finish reminiscent of its 1800s Windsor ancestor. The catalogue described it as "genuine early American style" and priced it at $4.55. By the late 1930s, rocking chairs declined in popularity because people preferred larger, overstuffed chairs.

In the 1960s, rocking chairs returned to the limelight when President John F. Kennedy touted their benefits for his ailing back. The President was frequently photographed in a tall-backed wooden rocker that previously was considered porch furniture.

Since the 1970s, these relics have not been eagerly collected except by truly savvy antiquers. Since antique rocking chairs are no longer considered trendy, they're real bargains. Before these wonderful antiques lose

Treadway Toomey Galleries

Here's a wonderful Gustav Stickley rocker, model #375, with original leather seat.

their comfy affordability, be on the lookout for just the right model. Then find a special spot, preferably on a hardwood or tile floor, (nevertheless do move it around to save wear and tear). There you can enjoy reading about antiques, or savor birds or flowers outside.

Du Mouchelle's Auction

The Stickley Brothers version of the rocking chair displays the characteristic slats and straight lines of the Arts and Crafts style.

Treadway Toomey Galleries

Gustav Stickley even made rocking chairs for small tykes. Imagine the joy this chair has witnessed.

Chapter 35

Windsor Chairs: History Meets Mass Production

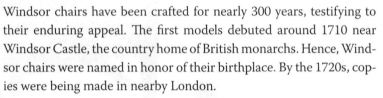

Windsor chairs have been crafted for nearly 300 years, testifying to their enduring appeal. The first models debuted around 1710 near Windsor Castle, the country home of British monarchs. Hence, Windsor chairs were named in honor of their birthplace. By the 1720s, copies were being made in nearby London.

Many collectors consider less cumbersome looking American Windsors superior to the English versions for several reasons. British chairs had a rather awkward central flat splat/backrest 3 to 4 inches wide surrounded on both sides by tubby spindles. American cabinet makers eliminated the splat/backrest, placed skinnier spindles all across the back, and made legs less bulky.

The low-key "country" look of Windsor chairs is somewhat misleading. In the early 1800s, they were an early success story for mass production. The rounded legs, stretchers, and spindles could easily be shaped on lathes in large quantities, while standardization made parts interchangeable. Cabinetmakers located all over the country ordered ready-made parts from Connecticut factories and then assembled and painted chairs in their workshops.

Parts for chairs were crafted from various woods. Seats were of soft pine, while legs and backs were usually built from stronger maple or oak. Chairs were ordinarily painted black or other colors to appear totally crafted from one timber. Green was especially chosen for porches and verandahs to match the verdant landscape of the outdoors. And cheerful yellow brightened dreary candlelit interiors before electric lighting.

Throughout a long history, Windsor chairs have served many uses in all parts of homes, including kitchens, guest rooms, porches and gardens. Occasionally, Windsors strayed into dining rooms when additional seating was needed for extra-large dinners. Whatever color,

Skinner Auctions, Inc.

Feast your eyes on various American Windsor chairs dating from 1780 to 1810.

Skinner Auctions, Inc.

These New England beauties are known as "Birdcage" and date to around 1809.

and whether solid splat or spindle back, they always looked mighty fine even among fancy mahogany pieces.

Windsor chairs are entwined with American history. For instance, Philadelphia cabinetmaker Francis Trumble (1716-1798) made 114 for the Philadelphia State House. Benjamin Franklin, Robert Morris, and other patriots rose from the recently installed Trumble-made Windsor chairs to sign the Declaration of Independence at Independence Hall on July 4, 1776.

Moreover, George and Martha Washington had several Windsor chairs on their columned front verandah, where they and their guests

Author's collection

Sears even offered a Retro version of the Windsor chair. enjoyed the view of the Potomac River that flowed in front of Mount Vernon. If you visit that captivating home, take a break and feel like 1700s gentry by sitting in early 1900s reproductions based on the Washington originals.

Can you believe that even a house designed by ultramodern architect Frank Lloyd Wright had Windsor chairs? Mr. Wright usually dictated furnishings for clients and rarely, if ever, did he include antiques. Sleek chrome kitchen stools reminiscent of the Bauhaus School would seem right at home in the high-tech 1930s kitchen of the magical Fallingwater house, an architectural masterpiece located south of Pittsburgh, Pennsylvania. But the home's original owners, the Kaufmanns, insisted on 1830s versions of the chairs gracing Mount Vernon and Independence Hall. They obviously recognized fine chair design. There is no better endorsement for Windsors!

This modern looking chair created by Hans Wegner of Denmark in the mid-20th century still has the 1700s Windsor look.

Skinner Auctions, Inc.

Chapter 36

Hitchcock Chairs: No Mystery about These Stenciled Treasures

The name Hitchcock is associated with chairs as well as classic movies. While Alfred Hitcock is famous for riveting mysteries, Lambert Hitchcock (1795-1852) is known for beautifully stenciled chairs. In 1821, Hitchcock established a manufacturing firm at the junction of the Farmington and Still Rivers in northwest Connecticut. This remote area offered plenty of lumber, an existing sawmill and water-power, but proved too far from cities, a needed source of labor and ready markets. Added to these hurdles, the horrendous New England winters made transportation of goods treacherous, since railroads were still uncommon.

Hitchcock managed to survive such drawbacks to create a major chapter in the history of the Industrial Revolution. The chair maker followed the lead of fellow Yankee artistic and business genius, Eli Terry, who designed inexpensive wooden works for clocks and even devised an assembly line process for cutting parts and assembling them.

Hitchcock used similar processes to make well-built, affordable chairs. His factory, like those of Windsor chair manufacturers, produced chairs in unassembled kits with interchangeable parts that could be economically transported and assembled later. Almost 175 years later, most new furniture is sold and shipped the same way, which proves that the furniture maker was well ahead of his time.

Hitchcock followed the designs of Sheraton and Hepplewhite, which at the time, were mighty fashionable. He relied on rounded (turned-on-lathe) legs for furniture that could easily be made in large quantities. He also limited costs using the recently developed British stenciling process, which was far swifter than hand carving. Stencils allowed fast decorating by applying multicolored metallic powders to wet varnish or paint. Fashionable neoclassical motifs such as leaves, flowers and baskets of fruit that embellished upscale Hepplewhite pieces were reproduced in stenciled designs.

Business flourished because Hitchcock chairs were reasonably priced at 50 cents to $1.50. In time, his town became known as Hitchcockville, which today is called Riverton. By 1825, Hitchcock had erected a three-story brick factory equipped with water-powered machinery, all 38 years before the birth of industrialist Henry Ford. Along with rocking chairs and settees, his firm produced as many as 300 Sheraton-type chairs per week.

A close look at a circa 1830s Hitchcock chair with rush seat.

Garth's Auctions, Inc.

Bright decorations of fruit or flowers on black, green or yellow chairs beautified cottages and frontier homes across America. Imagine the thrill for a 1820s housewife as her long-awaited Hitchcock chairs arrived in the then rough-and-tumble town of Chicago. No doubt they stood out where simpler furniture was the norm. Thanks to their high-end looks, Hitchcock chairs justifiably became known as fancy chairs.

The term "Hitchcock chair" eventually became a

generic name for any stenciled or painted chair that resembled Hitchcock originals. Consequently, Hitchcock distinguished his wares by stenciling them with the words "L. Hitchcock. Hitchcock-Ville, Conn. Warranted."

In 1829, Lambert Hitchcock's brother-in-law, Arba Alford (1807-1881) became a partner in the business. After Hitchcock died in 1852, the firm slumbered during the late 1800s and early 20th century, but the "Early American" decorating craze of the 1940s revived it. Hitchcock chairs personified "Early American," since they had been crafted nonstop since the early days of the country.

Today the Hitchcock Chair Company is alive and well and producing future antiques. Chairs still follow originals right down to labels. The modern company uses backward "N's," plus a registered trademark to subtly indicate a post-1946 production.

Antique Hitchcock chairs with their plank or rush seats are too small, rickety and uncomfortable for modern tastes that favor upholstered seats. This makes antique Hitchcock chairs very affordable. A beauty from the 1830s can go at auction for $150 to $200, but no doubt Hitchcock chairs will eventually escalate in value and become as pricey as early 1800s Windsor chairs.

Chapter 37

Dolls: The Most Joyous Antiques of All

The word "doll" comes from "eidolon," which in Greek means idol. In ancient societies, dolls were made for religious purposes. Later, Christians routinely used them for crèches at Christmas. In fact, Naples, Italy, became celebrated for miniature recreations of the birth of Christ. Dolls continued to be religious artifacts until about 1450, when to children's delight, they also became playthings. Early examples lacking any slick refinement were made from clay, stone, bone or wood.

By the mid-1700s, dolls became commonplace. In the next century, doll making shifted from cottage craft to factory production in Germany, France and England. Various materials including wood, composition (a material made from pulped wood), porcelain, wax and cloth were used in their manufacture.

During the 1840s, the "pull" doll was developed, featuring eyes that opened or closed by pulling on a wire that ran under clothing and through the neck to the head. Later methods used lead weights attached to the backs of the eyes.

This English Queen Anne doll, made from wood, dates to around 1735.

Doll making became so important that many countries exhibited wonderful examples at the very first world's fair. Touting the advances created by the Industrial Revolution, the Great Exhibition of 1851 held in London's Crystal Palace showcased dolls to the delight of both children and adults.

In the late 1800s, Dressel and Schilling of Germany were highly regarded for dolls with delicate porcelain heads. The famous French firm Jumeau created mechanical dolls that could even speak, and savvy English doll maker Augusta Montana created little tykes resembling Queen Victoria's children.

In the United States, dolls created before the Civil War were less sophisticated than their European counterparts. American makers were informally trained and used rustic materials such as wood, clothespins or rags. Dolls from this era today are prime examples of American Folk/Naïve Art.

A slightly later Queen Anne doll made around 1780.

Soon Yankee ingenuity caught up with European advances. In 1855, Benjamin Lee of New York made the first rubber doll, and a decade later another clever American crafted a celluloid model. These innovations made dolls more affordable for less privileged children.

During the decades after the American Civil War, both European and American dolls reflected lavish Victorian lifestyles. Dolls showcased real hair and sophisticated costumes of billowing skirts with bustles and bodices encased in colorful silks, satins and lace embellishments.

Skinner Auctions, Inc.

This fashionable young Parisian dating from 1860s retains her stylish wardrobe.

One particular doll, a true American icon, has brought endless joy to children and legendary status to its namesake. The original Ideal Toy Company introduced in the early 1900s an appealing version of the 1800s rag doll—the teddy bear, named after President Theodore Roosevelt.

Until 1900, dolls mostly portrayed girls or young ladies. In the United States around World War I, a revolutionary doll appeared. Grace Putnam Storey created a doll named the "Bye-lo Baby," modeled after a real three-day-old baby. It became a mega hit and remains so among collectors even today. This led to the 1930s movie star Shirley Temple and the Canadian Dionne quintuplets becoming models. And, once again, doll history repeated itself. Just as in the previous century when royal children had been models for a shrewd toy maker, so was the future Queen Elizabeth II of Great Britain. In the days when the young Princess was known as "Lillibet," her replica was marketed right down to her nickname.

In the early 20th century, plastic transformed doll making. "Dydee"

A fine example of the famous American Greiner papier-mâché doll from 1850.

This French beauty was made between 1860 and 1870. The painted bisque (unglazed porcelain) head was made by Huret.

was an early plastic model that could drink from a bottle and wet her diapers. Shortly afterwards, the doll stork delivered a lifelike "Tiny Tears," which became immensely popular.

For many doll devotees, the most famous example is the iconic Barbie, who made her ever-so-chic debut in 1958. This American princess became so adulated that Mattel Toys marketed Ken to create a little romance. When the firm publicized that the couple had a parting of the ways, the shocking news created as much hoopla as when Lucille Ball divorced Desi Arnaz in the late 1950s. Such is the steadfast appeal of dolls.

Marks on dolls, usually found on the rear of the head, neck or back, help identify maker and age. *Warman's Antiques and Collectibles Price Guide* offers much information and a good idea of values. Keep in mind that the tips your antiques coach gave you for dating china also work well with dolls.

An ever joyful spin-off from dolls is the dollhouse. Dollhouses made in the 1700s were elaborate miniature replicas of homes. Early models were equipped with Chippendale and Hepplewhite furnishings. Replicas from the late 1800s repeated Victorian flamboyancy in minute detail, including gilding and ornate furnishings.

A most extraordinary dollhouse—or more accurately, a doll cas-

Skinner Auctions, Inc.

This stylish 1830s German lass is a three-dimensional paper figure dressed in a handmade tissue costume.

This 1830s French paper doll has quite a range of outfits in her trousseau.

tle—awaits your viewing at the Museum of Science and Industry in Chicago's Hyde Park. This glorious palace even has a regal set of English Royal Doulton china. No wonder this miniature masterpiece cost $500,000 in 1935. What pleasure this petite chateau has given visitors since early film star Colleen Moore bequeathed it.

You might wonder about the secret to the huge following for antique dolls and their homes. Even though many sell for thousands, money has little to do with their allure. Passionate collectors will readily declare that they are driven by sentimentality. All the accumulated pleasure that long-ago children enjoyed from these treasures has been bestowed upon current guardians.

SECTION SIX

Preparing for Graduation

Chapter 38
Future Antiques

As I have mentioned before, the definition of antiques keeps changing, but that's to our benefit. That became apparent to me in class one day. After a lecture, a gentleman once asked me, "Do they still make antiques?" Believe it or not, until then, the thought had never occurred to me. His marvelous question helped me realize that, thankfully, antiques are still being made, and because more items qualify as antiques every year, new generations will have sufficient supplies. In the 22nd century, antiques will include quality items being created today, such as handmade quilts, hooked rugs and, no doubt, post-Retro versions of "El on Vel."

This art glass lamp made by Charles Lotton in 1993 is already on its way to becoming a future antique.

Early Auction Company

World famous
Murano Art Glass
of Florence, Italy,
is making future
antiques such as this
sculptured vase by
Lino Tagliapietra.

Another future
antique by
Charles Lotton
in 1994 would
please even
Mr. Tiffany.

Early Auction Company

Early Auction Company

Chapter 39

Raising the Antiques Roof

You're about to graduate from Antiques 101, but before I send you out on your antiques adventure, I want to share with you a wonderful story I hope will inspire you.

Tim Tyler and his wife, Kathy, live in suburban Cincinnati on a street full of upscale houses all about 20 years old. When looking at the Williamsburg-type residences in the neighborhood, antiques aren't the first things that come to mind. Interiors are more likely decorated with reproductions of 1700s Queen Anne and Chippendale styles.

But unlike its neighbors, Tyler Manor (as I affectionately call the family's home) doesn't follow a Williamsburg design. Rather, exposed exterior wooden beams and a generous amount of stucco duplicate English houses built during the reign of Henry Tudor.

In 2003, Tim's in-laws, Kay and Bill Hauer, were leaving their downtown townhouse for a retirement cottage. Kathy's parents, having lived an antiques lifestyle, rarely bought anything brand

Tim and Kathy Tyler stand in front of the Berkey and Gay dresser handed down from Kathy's great-grandfather William Scully, who ordered a suite after falling in love with the one displayed at the Centennial Exposition of 1876.

new. Their house was full of great grandpa's desk or grandmother's china, or in other words, every collector's dream. When I visited them just before they moved, I asked who would be the lucky new owner of the bedroom suite, a special heirloom that had been in the family for more than 125 years.

This treasured keepsake dates to when the United States celebrated the 100th Anniversary of the signing of the Declaration of Independence. In honor of the momentous event, the Centennial Exposition, akin to a world's fair, was held in 1876. The Philadelphia exhibition highlighted technological wonders such as telegraphs and telephones, but one extremely popular display kindled the fervor for collecting antiques. Remember how Wallace Nutting loved the "Olde Tyme" presentation that highlighted Colonial relics in

Tim does repair and restoration work while Samantha looks on.

Tim and Kathy's meticulous work preserved the set for future generations.

a mocked-up Colonial kitchen?

Bedroom furniture presented in another of the exposition's many halls was the last word in stylishness in the 1870s. This stunning set, made by world famous Berkey and Gay Company of Grand Rapids, Michigan, loomed as high and as ornately as medieval Gothic cathedrals. Today its style as you now know, is called Renaissance Revival, or as I like to say, Medieval Revival, which accurately defines its trademarks. In the 21st century, this same suite is on display in the Public Museum of Grand Rapids.

Family lore had always claimed that when Bill Hauer's maternal grandfather, William Scully, visited the Philadelphia Exposition, he fell in love with the displayed suite and ordered one for his home.

Attention to detail is essential in doing quality work that will stand the test of time.

Grandpa Scully's bedroom furniture consisted of a bed, a dresser with mirror, a nightstand and a washstand with fitted porcelain sink compete with faucet. In 1876, a washstand fitted with a sink was considered quite high tech and revealed that Grandma and Grandpa Scully had indoor plumbing in the days when such equipment was not the norm.

So when Kay told me that her son-in-law and daughter were taking Grandpa Scully's suite, I was thrilled. (In my appraisal work, I always urge families to keep heirlooms.) I blurted, "Oh, I guess they live in an old house with high ceilings." Kay replied with a chuckle, "No, my

The Tylers modified their roof trusses to raise the ceiling in their bedroom to accommodate the massive furniture.

The finished ceiling beautifully accentuates the furniture and makes room for the nearly 10-foot-tall pieces.

son-in-law is raising the ceiling of their bedroom to accommodate the bed and dresser."

Why did the suite appeal to Tim? He said, "The sheer grandeur! I've never seen a suite quite as elaborate. There are both massive sections and finely carved areas. It is made of American walnut veneer with solid carvings and moldings. The bed stands just over 9 feet tall and the dresser is slightly less than 10 feet high."

Tim didn't strip and refinish the suite, because he felt that would be a sin. He wanted to maintain the patina, which is the natural shading that accumulates around carvings and handles over many years. Tim cleaned and glued loose carvings, including several almost three-dimensionally carved cherubs. He restored the natural finish with Howard's Restore-A-Finish, which gently cleans and polishes the finish already present. He then coated the finish with paste wax to preserve the beautiful aged look I like to call "the kiss of time." (The technique Tim used is explained in detail in Chapter 14 of *Secrets to Affordable Antiques*.) Tim also removed the ceiling in the bedroom and modified the roof trusses to create room for the towering bedroom set.

Tim and Kathy chose to carefully restore the natural finish rather than stripping and refinishing it, which would have destroyed more than 100 years of patina.

Meanwhile, Kathy selected lovely striped wallpaper to give the room a fitting Victorian ambience.

Kathy recreated the layer-upon-layer look of Gilded Age window treatments with these curtains.

Almost a year after the Tylers began the project, I visited them to see their progress. Between sips of champagne, I rubbed my hands all over the numerous carvings on the bed, washstand and chest of drawers. How pleased I am that Kathy and Tim never refinished, but rather restored the set. It still has nicks and scratches all over, but what else should we expect? It is 130 years old and is bound to be kissed by time. Grandpa Scully's bedroom furniture is antique and looks beautifully old. Cheers to Tim and Kathy's hard work!

The striped wallpaper brings out the colors of the set's dark walnut wood. Kathy managed to find curtains at J.C. Penney and did a terrific job of recreating the layer upon layer look of Gilded Age window treatments.

Everyone at Tyler Manor is pleased with Grandpa Scully's suite, including the Tylers' daughters of the human, as well as the canine variety. Samantha and Ginger, the two dogs, sleep behind the high headboard at night. Remember when we talked about antiques and Feng Shui? Well, this set has all the good vibes. Kathy says it is so quiet to sleep in the bed, "it's almost like cave." Then she told me why. "When I

The striped wallpaper brings out the color of the suite's dark walnut wood.

was a little girl and had nightmares, I would climb into my mom and dad's bed to get over my nightmare," she said.

When I talked to Tim about four months before finishing, he was rather frustrated and tired with this huge endeavor. But when I asked him if he would do it again, he replied, "Oh, yes, without a doubt."

Keep in mind this account of two people's passion about antiques to inspire you. Never once did Tim mention the set's monetary value. Grandpa Scully's furniture has made Tim an antiquer extraordinaire, not collecting for financial reward but rather for the delight antiques bring. Always remember the joy antiques bring to our lives and you will do as grandly as my friends Tim and Kathy Tyler.

The bed's imposing headboard features three-dimensional
hand-carved cherubs and other finely detailed decorative work.

Now the time has come for you to graduate from Antiques 101! Congratulations, and let your antiques coach bid you a fond au revoir by saying as I love to do: "Keep Antiquing!"

Bibliography

Aikman, Lonelie. *The Living White House*, revised edition. Washington, D.C.: National Geographic Society, 1987.

Aldridge, Eileen. *Porcelain*. New York: Grosset and Dunlap, 1970.

Bates, Elizabeth Bidwell, and Jonathan L. Fairbanks. *American Furniture 1620 to Present*. New York: Richard Marek, 1981.

Beck, Doreen. *The Book of American Furniture*. London, England: Hamlyn, 1973.

Bishop, Robert, Judith Wessman, Michael McManus, and Harry Nieman, *Folk Art Paintings, Sculpture, and Country Objects*. New York: Alfred A. Knopf, 1983.

Blair, James Jr. "Sharing a Life by Design." Christian Science Monitor, Jan. 3, 2000, Vol. 93, Issue 27, p. 15.

Boger, Louise Ade. *The Complete Guide to Furniture Styles*. New York: Charles Scribner's Sons, 1959.

Brunt, Andrew. *Phaidon Guide to Furniture*. Englewood Cliffs, N.J.: Prentice Hall, 1983.

Bury, Shirley. *Victorian Electroplate*. Country Life Collectors' Guide. Hamlyn, 1971.

Butler, Joseph T. *American Antiques 1800-1900, A Collector's History and Guide*. Odyssey Press, 1965.

Carron, Christian. *Grand Rapids Furniture*. Grand Rapids, Mich.: The Public Museum of Grand Rapids, 1998.

Chippendale, Thomas. *The Gentleman and Cabinet-Maker's Director*, a reprint of the 3rd edition. New York: Dover Publications, 1966.

Cole, Ann Kilborn. *Antiques: How to Identify, Buy, Sell, Refinish and Care for Them*. New York: Collier Books, 1962.

Daniel, Dorothy. *Cut and Engraved Glass: 1771-1905, The Collector's Guide to American Wares*. New York: M. Barrows and Company, 6th edition, 1950.

Delieb, Eric. *Investing in Silver*. New York: Clarkson N. Potter, 1967.

Drepperd, Carl W. *The Primer of American Antiques*. Garden City, New York: Doubleday and Company, Inc., 1944.

Ellis, Anita. *Rookwood Pottery, the Glorious Gamble*. New York: Rizzoli, 1992.

Garet, Barbara. "Heywood-Wakefield Revisited." Wood & Wood Products, April 1995, V100 no. 5 p 26 (4).

Garrett, Elizabeth Donaghy. *The American Family 1750 to 1870*. New York: Harry N. Abrams, 1989.

Godden, Geoffrey A. *Encyclopedia of British Pottery and Porcelain Marks*. New York, 1964.

Goldsmith, Diane. "Exhibit Showcases Designer's Colorful Plan for Living." Philadelphia Enquirer, Jan. 10, 2002.

Greene, Jeffrey P. *American Furniture of the 18th Century.* Newtown, Conn.: Taunton Press, 1996.

Grotz, George. *The Furniture Doctor.* New York: Doubleday and Company, 1962.

Hageman, Jane Sikes and Edward M. *Ohio Furniture Makers*, volumes 1 and 2. Cincinnati, Ohio, 1989.

Hammerton, John. *The Illustrated World History.* New York: Wm. H. Wise and Company, 1935.

Higgins and Seiter China and Cut Glass, 1899. Princeton, New Jersey: Pyne Press, 1971.

Howe, Jennifer L., editor, *Cincinnati Art-Carved Furniture and Interiors.* Cincinnati Art Museum, Cincinnati: Ohio University Press, 2003.

Hughes, Bernard and Therle. *The Collector's Encyclopedia of English Ceramics.* Abbey Library, 1968.

Husfloen, Kyle. *Collector's Guide to American Pressed Glass.* 1825-1915, Radnor, Pennsylvania: Wallace Homestead, 1992.

Kerfoot, J.B. *American Pewter.* New York: Crown Publishers, 1942.

Kert, Bernice. *Abby Aldrich Rockefeller.* Random House, 1993.

Kinard, Epsie. *The Care and Keeping of Antiques.* New York: Hawthorn Books, 1971.

Laver, James. *Edwardian Promenade.* Houghton Mifflin Company, 1958.

Lee, Ruth Webb. *Victorian Glass.* Published by the author, 1944.

Linquist, David P., and Caroline C. Warren. *Victorian Furniture with Prices.* Radnor, Pennsylvania: Wallace Homestead, 1995.

MacKay, James. *An Encyclopedia of Small Antiques.* New York: Harper and Row, 1975.

McClinton, Katharine Morrison. *Collecting American 19th Century Silver.* New York: Bonanza Books, 1968.

Muller, R. Charles and Timothy D. Rieman. *The Chair, Illustrations: Stephen Metzger Canal.* Winchester, Ohio: Canal Press, 1984.

Nichols, Frederick D. and James A. Bear, Jr. *Monticello, A Guidebook.* Monticello, Virginia: Thomas Jefferson Memorial Foundation, 1982.

Okie, Howard Pitcher. *Old Silver and Old Sheffield Plate.* New York: Doubleday and Company, 1928.

Osborn, Howard. *An Illustrated Companion to the Decorative Arts.* Wordsworth Editions, Oxford University Press, 1975.

Papert, Emma. *The Illustrated Guide to American Glass.* New York: Hawthorn Books, 1972.

Philips, Phoebe, ed., *The Collector's Encyclopedia of Antiques*. New York: Crown Publishers, 1973.

Rainwater, Dorothy T. *Encyclopedia of American Silver Manufacturers*. New York: Crown Publishers, 1978.

Robertson, R.A. *Old Sheffield Plate*. Fair Lawn, New Jersey: Essential Books, 1957.

Robsjohn-Gibbings, T. H. *Good-bye, Mr. Chippendale*. New York: Alfred Knopf, 1944.

Roulard, Steven and Linda. *Knoll Furniture 1938-1960*. Atglen, Penn.: Schiffer, 2004.

Saarinen, Aline B. *The Proud Possessors*. New York: Random House, 1958.

Santore, Charles. *The Windsor Style In America*, volumes I and II. Philadelphia: Running Press, 1992.

Sikes, Jane E. (Hageman) *The Furniture Makers of Cincinnati 1790-1840*. Cincinnati, 1976.

Stickley, George. *Stickley Craftsman Furniture Catalogs, Unabridged Reprints of Two Mission Furniture Catalogs*, "Craftsman Furniture Made by Gustav Stickley" and "The works of L. and J.G. Stickley," New York: Dover Publications, 1979.

Stone, Jonathan. *English Silver of the 18th Century*. London: Cory Adams and MacKay Ltd. 1965.

Stout, Sandra McPhee. *Depression Glass Price Guide*. Des Moines, Iowa: Wallace Homestead, 1976.

Strong, Roy, *The Random House Collector's Encyclopedia: Victorian to Art Deco*. New York: Random Hose, 1974.

"Collectibles." Toronto Star, March 10, 2002.

Walton, Paul. *Renoir*. New York: Tudor Publishing, 1967.

Watson, Aldren A. *Country Furniture*. Lyons & Burford, 1974.

Wenham, Edward. *Antiques A to Z*. London: G. Bell and Sons, 1969.

Williams, Peter. *Wedgwood, A Collector's Guide*. Radnor, Penn.: Chilton, 1992.

Willis, Geoffrey. *Wedgwood*. Secaucus, N.J.: Charwell Books, 1989.

Index

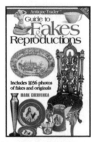

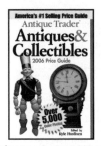

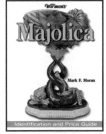